TOUGH TIMES
DON'T LAST

BY

TIM GILLIGAN

DEDICATION

To my family . . . Alicia, Lee and Katie (and Gavin), Alyce, Joshua, Greta and Gabriel. In tough times and in the best of times, you — my family — are my greatest treasure. Your love and support, plus the joy and strength you bring me, make me the most blessed man I know!

© 2010 by Tim Gilligan

Meadowbrook Church

4741 S.W. 20th Street • Ocala, FL 34474

www.mbcocala.com

ISBN 978-0-615-41279-5

All rights reserved. No part of this book may be reproduced in any form or by any electronic or mechanical means, including information storage and retrieval systems, without permission in writing from the publisher, except by a reviewer who may quote brief passages in a review.

Unless otherwise indicated, all Scripture quotations are taken from the *New King James Version* (*NKJV*), © 1979, 1980, 1982 by Thomas Nelson, Inc. Used by permission.

Scripture quotations marked *Message* are taken from *The Message Bible* by Eugene H. Peterson, © 1993 by NavPress.

Scripture quotations marked *NLT* are taken from the *New Living Translation*, © 2004 by Tyndale House.

Scripture quotations marked *AMP* are taken from the *Amplified Bible*, © 1987 by Zondervan Publishing House.

Edited by Cynthia McFarland

Cover Design by Lee Gilligan

Typesetting by Kate Riordan

TABLE OF CONTENTS

INTRODUCTION

"God help me!"

If you've ever said this in a frantic, stressful moment, you're not alone. It's certainly a common prayer, and one God is eager to answer, but do you actually understand how to incorporate His help into your life? Do some difficulties seem to linger and make you weary?

Relationship struggles, financial challenges, health concerns, and family problems are part of living in this world. From your own address, to the neighborhood around you, to the nation, to some far-off land, fears and problems are no longer limited by distance. Technology and travel have reduced this vast earth to a global community. Now every individual feels and/or deals with the fallout of both macro and micro issues and challenges.

Paul dealt with some of these same challenges as he wrote in 2 Corinthians.7:5 (NKJV), "We faced conflict from every direction, with battles on the outside and fear on the inside."

When the pressures of life are closing in on all sides, it often seems there is no escape. Tough times are a reality, but they don't have to dominate your existence, and they don't have to last indefinitely.

When you understand how to properly equip yourself with God's Word and His powerful principles, you'll be able to deal with trials and come through with a testimony that will strengthen you and bless those around you. You can stand firm in the face of life's challenges.

Further, by reviewing and adjusting your perspective from a scriptural view, you will find that these problems, or "tough times," actually are *not* the main issue. They seem to be a constant in life, no matter who you are or where you live. But they are subject to a number of principles and practices, as well as the promises and power of God.

In over thirty years of ministry I have come to realize that much of ministry is actually "people repair." Whether from wrong choices, lack of instruction, setbacks, careless or wicked people, or just from traveling through this life, people incur damage. They suffer damage to their souls, their relationships and their dreams. Thankfully, we have a good shepherd Who restores our souls, shows us a better way, and promises to accompany us through any tough times that we may come across.

The book you hold in your hands first began as a six-week teaching series on Sunday mornings at Meadowbrook Church. When it quickly became one of our most popular, most requested series ever, I felt God leading us to make it available as a book. I pray it will bless you and provide biblically sound, useful tools to ensure that tough times don't become routine in your life. There is light at the end of the tunnel!

Grace and Peace,

Tim Gilligan

The righteous person faces many troubles,

but the LORD comes to the rescue each time.

(Psalm 34:19 NLT-SE)

Here's a simple prayer you can pray
asking God to help you get more
out of your time with Him.

Heavenly Father, let the light of Your Word

shine down into the dark places of my heart.

Let the promises of Your Word encourage my soul.

Let the truth of Your Word reshape my attitudes.

And let the wisdom of Your Word

guide my decisions.

CHAPTER 1

TOUGH TIMES: A PART OF LIFE

In this world, one thing is certain: there will be tough times. No one is immune to the pressures, problems and challenges of life. At some point, troubling family situations, difficult relationships, financial ups and downs, and health issues come into every life.

In Matthew 5:45, Jesus said the Father makes the sun rise on the wicked and on the good, and makes the rain fall on both the just and unjust. Good things happen to bad people and bad things happen to good people. It's part of living on this earth.

But while tough times come to everybody, the good news is, those tough times don't have to last. If you're not properly equipped, however, tough times can stick around a lot longer than you'd like. They can even go from bad to worse. Perhaps a better title for this book is, *Tough Times Don't Have to Last.*

People often make decisions that actually extend and intensify their troubles. They may also have spiritual, emotional or mental conditions that prolong hard times. If you're uninformed, or misinformed, if you're ill-equipped, if you lack strength, if you make wrong decisions, or if you're headed in the wrong direction, those tough times can linger.

Sometimes we find ourselves in tough times that are of our own making, where the situation is one that we've created — whether intentionally or by accident. Proverbs 11:29 talks about one who troubles his/her own house, and Proverbs 14:1 says there's one who tears down his/her own house. Sadly, we can mess up our own lives — and negatively impact those around us — when our priorities are wrong or unbalanced, or when there are strongholds in our lives. We can literally trouble and tear down our own lives.

In other instances, tough times are individual situations that we didn't create or put in motion. Like it or not, the reality is that some things come into our lives that are not our fault. They happen simply because we live in a fallen, broken world. We have to deal with those times even though we didn't cause them and don't deserve them.

Tough times come and often affect a large number of people. In 2004, several dangerous hurricanes hit the Southeastern United States and impacted many people. For some, their lives were changed forever. For others, the storms were just major inconveniences.

During that memorable September, I realized firsthand that preparation directly affects how *long* tough times last.

When the first hurricane came through, our electricity was out for seven or eight days. We had a little generator but it couldn't handle much, so I was constantly getting up through the night refueling the generator and checking the oil to keep it going.

By the time storm number two hit later that month, I had me a big ole "mama" generator! I was prepared! I was equipped! This new generator was hooked up to natural gas and a mere seventeen seconds after the electricity went out, that generator switched on, and I started proclaiming, "Thank you, Jesus, for technology!"

The little generator was better than nothing, but that big, powerful generator was *much* better! Just like the old fairy tale of the three little pigs, you can choose to build your house out of sticks, hay, or brick. **Preparation is everything.**

The economy is another area where preparation is crucial for surviving tough times. If you manage to save and build up some margin, you won't have the same pressure as those who are living paycheck to paycheck with a zero balance in their savings account. **More margin equals less pressure.**

There are a variety of reasons why negative things come into our lives, and we'll address how to handle this in later chapters, but for now, let's consider how we perceive trouble.

There's always a **perception of degree** when problems arise. Some people — I guarantee you know at least one or two — always want to claim the "honor" of having the worst troubles in life. Their negative mindset is always focused on the dark side of every situation. If you have something tough happening in your life, they have something twice as tough. If you're dealing with a bad situation, you can be sure whatever they're dealing with is much worse... at least in their eyes.

Perception of degree actually refers to the fact that there is always someone, somewhere, who's worse off than you. No matter how bad things seem, you are always better off than someone else. Once you realize this, it will help you avoid getting caught up in a destructive "woe is me" mentality. People have a tendency to be negative and negativity left unchecked spreads very quickly.

If you look at global statistics, you'll quickly realize we are in pretty good shape just because we live in America. Forgive me for being positive! The truth is, it's not what happens to you that matters. What matters is what you do with what happens to you.

I want to give you an important principle to follow... **your outlook determines your outcome.** Let's look at this a little closer.

Your attitude is your frame of mind. Your attitude (frame of mind) determines your approach, which refers to the methods you use to handle situations. Your approach determines your success or your failure.

"Your outlook determines your outcome; your attitude determines your approach, and your approach determines your success or your failure," says Pastor A. R. Bernard, pastor of Christian Cultural Center, a Brooklyn, New York-based church with over 30,000 members.

Because of this truth, it's very important that we guard our attitudes. For example, we must be careful about getting offended. When someone gets offended about something, he won't be led by the Holy Spirit. Instead of being led the way the Holy Spirit guides, he'll be led by offense. Whenever we're led by anything other than the Holy Spirit, we're going to end up in the wrong place. So we need to guard our attitudes.

We must also guard our outlook concerning all things because this affects what we do next. Again, your outlook determines your outcome. There's only one thing you can control (the control freaks won't like this, but it's true), and that's your thinking.

Whenever we're led by anything other than the Holy Spirit, we're going to end up in the wrong place. So we need to guard our attitudes.

When someone says, "I can't control my thoughts," they probably haven't tried. They're so accustomed to letting television, the media, other people and emotions guide their thinking, but every individual ultimately has control over what he or she thinks.

Granted, we all need to work on this area. So often we have the tendency to become negative or hopeless, but when we start going down that road, we need to stop and remind ourselves: I can control my thinking. 2 Corinthians 10:5 tells us that we can take our thoughts captive and cast down imaginations. There are definite ways that we can control our thoughts and it's vital that we guard what we allow to enter our minds.

There are three important things we need to remember about tough times.

1. Don't be Surprised

The first is that we shouldn't be surprised by tough times. On average, 25 percent of your day is hard and/or unpleasant. We need to accept this fact from the beginning and cherish the days when the difficult times are less than 25 percent.

Even if you head to Disney World, "the happiest place on earth," you can be sure at some point you're going to encounter someone *goofy* who will put a damper on your day... and I don't mean the Goofy who works there!

There will always be a mix of things throughout the day that are difficult and/or unpleasant. It's just part of living in this world. It's not God turning His back on you. It's not a curse on you. It's just part of everyday life. Some events are beyond your control. It's not necessarily your fault that you got stuck in traffic on the way to work, or that you got a flat tire on the way home. Some days are clearly worse than others, but every day contains something unpleasant. Just acknowledge this: you can "carry your own weather with you" every day.

Instead of fretting because traffic is crawling along, pop in a CD of some uplifting music or a positive message. Be prepared so that whatever comes along, you can carry your own weather with you. The devil constantly tries to set you up to get you upset. It's one of his favorite tactics. If you've already made the decision to trust God and carry your own weather with you, the devil won't catch you off guard.

The other day I came home and didn't have a lot of time to spare. As I walked through the laundry room, I noticed my wife Alicia's little dog had left a series of "presents" all around the laundry room. Do I need to explain any further? And I thought, "UGHHHH."

Alicia and I have a rule that we've maintained throughout our marriage. As each of our five kids went through the diaper stage, the rule was "finders keepers." That little agreement carries over for pets, too. Was I going to gripe and complain and be mad? I reminded myself that I *carry my own weather with me*, and you guessed it... I cleaned it up!

If anyone told you that when you give your life to Jesus you will no longer have problems, they were either lying to you, or they were talking about heaven. As long as we're on this earth, we're going to encounter tough times.

In John 16:33 (AMP), Jesus said, "*I have told you these things so that in Me you may have [perfect] peace and confidence. In the world you have tribulation and trials and distress and frustration; but be of good cheer [take courage; be confident, certain, undaunted]! For I have overcome the world. [I have deprived it of power to harm you and have conquered it for you.]"*

Jesus says, *"Be of good cheer."* This means we have a decision to make. We can either be of good cheer... or not. It's our choice. We control how we react to what happens to us.

James 1:2 (NKJV) says, "My brethren, count it all joy **when** you fall into various trials." Notice it doesn't say "**if** you fall into various trials."

In Jeremiah 17:7-8 (NKJV) we read, "Blessed is the man who trusts in the Lord and whose hope is in the Lord. For he shall be like a tree planted by the waters, which spreads out its roots by the river, and will not fear when heat comes...."

Heat comes... hard times come... tough times come. This is a given in life. But the man who trusts in the Lord "will not fear when heat comes, but its leaf will be green, and will not be anxious in the year of drought, nor will cease, from yielding fruit."

In our church we have a saying: "Stay on the right side of the 'but.'" Some people have it the other way around and say, "I know the Bible says God will supply all my needs, **but** things sure look bad now. I don't know how I can get out of this mess." They're on the wrong side of the "but"!

We need to stay on the right side and say, "Things may look bad now and this really is a mess, **but** my God will supply all my needs according to His riches in glory by Christ Jesus!"

Yes, problems are a part of the human experience, **but** God has promised that if we trust in Him, we need not fear when difficulties arise. He gives us the power through the Holy Spirit to "be of good cheer," to control ourselves and take charge of our emotions.

Here's my point: tough times don't last. The enemy of your soul and the media would like to give you the perception that tough times are here to stay. They say it's all doom and gloom and it's only getting worse. Go back and do a little research; check out the headlines from one hundred years ago. The mindset is still the same. It's the nature of news and it's the nature of the enemy of your soul to make you think tough times are here to stay.

The truth is, if you don't handle things in the right way, they can stick around. If you're not properly equipped, they can get worse. But get hold of this: TOUGH TIMES DON'T LAST. There is a light at the end of the tunnel.

Proverbs 11:8 declares that God delivers the righteous out of trouble. There may be trouble, or tough times, but it won't last. Life is made up of seasons. A season is a period of time. Ecclesiastes 3:1-8 tells us that for everything there is a season. Every season takes its turn, and every season comes to an end. No winter lasts forever and no spring skips its turn.

2. You Will Come Through

The second thing you need to remember about tough times is that you can bear up under it. It's not more than you can bear. Just knowing that negative things won't last and that you will come through should give you hope.

A number of years ago, when I was going through a pretty hard time, someone told me, "You will always remember the pain, but you won't always feel the pain."

That was a valuable lesson. We've got to learn to separate the experience from the memory. All of us have endured times in our lives when we've felt incredible pain and feared that it would take us down and destroy us. Yet somehow, through a combination of God, time and wisdom, we plowed through and came out on the other side. We will never forget the pain, but thank God, we no longer feel it.

There are some people, however, who choose to hold onto pain. They act as though everything that's ever hurt them is still causing pain. Forget it. Let go!

1 Corinthians 10:13 (NKJV) says, "No temptation has overtaken you except such as is common to man...."

You don't have some unique situation that no one else has ever experienced. What you're going through is common to man; it's been experienced before.

That verse continues, "but God *is faithful, Who will not allow you to be* tempted beyond what you are able, but with the temptation (that test, that trial, that adversity), will also make the way of escape that you may be able to bear it."

In the New Living Translation this same verse reads, "The temptations in your life are no different from what others experience. And God is faithful. He will not allow the temptation to be more than you can stand. When you are tempted, He will show you a way out so that you can endure."

Yes, problems are a part of the human experience, but God has promised that if we trust in Him, we need not fear when difficulties arise.

The Amplified Bible goes on to say, "For no temptation (no trial regarded as enticing to sin, no matter how it comes or where it leads) has overtaken you and laid hold on you that is not common to man [that is, no temptation or trial has come to you that is beyond human resistance and that is not adjusted and adapted and belonging to human experience, and such as man can bear]."

God is never the cause of pain in your life, but He does allow some things to happen. Even in our trials, we can find comfort in knowing that God has adjusted and adapted the situation to fit where we are in life. There are some things a child can bear and there are some things that a man can bear. Bleak as the situation might seem at the moment, it won't always be that bad.

God is faithful. Tough times don't last forever. You will make it through. Be assured of these truths, and don't speak otherwise. Never speak against your own hope.

So many times people speak negative things. This is understandable when you're going through a trial, but you must remember... despair and negative speaking are exactly what the enemy of your soul wants to hear. He's just looking for one more thing that will throw you over the edge. Don't give him the satisfaction! Instead, you need to speak OUT LOUD about the faithfulness of God.

Lord, I know what the world says, but I'm looking to You. I agree with David who wrote in Psalm 27:1b (NKJV), "The Lord is the strength of my life; of whom shall I be afraid?"

3. Strength is the Issue

The third thing we must remember is that strength is the issue… not the problem.

Proverbs 24:10 (NKJV) is really the foundational passage for this topic. It says, "If you faint in the day of adversity, your strength is small." In The Message Bible we read, "If you fall to pieces in a crisis, there wasn't much to you in the first place." This same verse in The New Living Translations says, "If you fail under pressure, your strength is too small."

Many people want to make the problem the issue. It's not hard to do when you have a bad day and listen to the news, but we must grasp the fact that the problem is not the issue, *strength is the issue*.

Not long ago, an elderly woman in Beaverton, Oregon, made the news on Fox 12 Oregon (Portland News). She lived on the second floor of an apartment building and had a hard time getting around by herself. The downstairs neighbor said he would often help her up and down the stairs, and carry her groceries.

The woman's daughter became concerned when she didn't hear from her mother. She kept calling the apartment, but her mother never answered the phone. Finally, the daughter contacted the apartment complex manager and asked him to check on her mother. The manager heard a faint noise from inside when he went to knock on the door. It was the elderly woman crying out for help. After breaking down the door, rescuers found the poor woman lying in the bathtub where she had been for the past five days. Taking a bath literally became a matter of life and death because the woman lacked strength to climb out of the tub.

Strength is the issue… not the problem!

On occasion, I do a ride-along with a sheriff's deputy. On one of these outings, we came upon a large dually truck that had gone off the road and a tow truck was called to pull it out. When the tow truck arrived, however, it was smaller than the dually. The driver of the tow truck took one look at the situation and announced, "We have a problem."

The little tow truck wasn't powerful enough to pull the dually back onto the road, so they had to call a bigger tow truck. The problem wasn't the issue, strength was the issue. If you faint in the day of adversity your strength is small. But if your strength is proportionate and able to handle the circumstances, then there is no problem.

If you're always centered on the problem, then you will always be looking to the problem. You need to stop focusing on the problem. Whatever you focus on will dominate your life. You need to find wise ways to increase your *strength* to deal with the problem. Once you tap into that strength, the problem will no longer be the focus.

Proverbs 18:14 (AMP) says, "The strong spirit of a man sustains him in bodily pain or trouble, but a weak and broken spirit who can raise up or bear?" The same verse in the Message Bible reads, "A healthy spirit conquers adversity, but what can you do when the spirit is crushed?"

A strong spirit sustains you. On the other hand, if your spirit is weak, broken, offended or crushed, you're in trouble! The strength of spirit that we're talking about is on the inside. It must be on the inside. You've got to be stronger on the inside than the problem on the outside. You won't cave in if you have more strength on the inside than there is pressure on the outside.

2 Timothy 2:1 (AMP) says, "So you, my son, be strong (strengthened inwardly) in the grace (spiritual blessing) that is [to be found only] in Christ Jesus."

This strength comes from God. It's called grace. Grace works on the inside and strengthens you inwardly, which is where you need it.

We all know what it's like to receive bad news and suddenly we just feel weak on the inside. You've got to have grace, dominant and abundant, in your life. That grace can only be found through trust in Christ Jesus.

James 4:6 (AMP) says, "But He gives us more and more grace (power of the Holy Spirit, to meet this evil tendency and all others fully). That is why He says, God sets Himself against the proud and haughty, but gives grace [continually] to the lowly (those who are humble enough to receive it)."

On your own, you don't have the strength to handle the tough times in life, but guess what? There is strength found only in the grace of our Lord Jesus. That strength, that grace, will flow into your inner being and build you

This strength comes from God. It's called grace. Grace works on the inside and strengthens you inwardly, which is where you need it.

up if you're humble enough to receive it. Talk about a good deal! He doesn't give grace to those who take a twelve-week class. He doesn't give it to those who behaved well for four days or got up early in the morning. He gives it to those who are humble enough to receive it.

This is why we need to declare, "God, You are the strength of my life! I need Your strength, I need Your grace to work inside me and strengthen me. It's supernatural and I'll take it! I can't fully explain it or understand all of it, but sign me up. I believe it, I need it, and it comes only from You."

You can't get grace anywhere else. He's the God of all grace, and He'll give more and more and more — a continuous flow of grace — to those who are humble enough to receive it. The Lord is your strength. I want you to get a revelation of this and grab hold of this truth: no matter what you're dealing with, the Lord gives you the strength that you need!

Proverbs 24:5 (NKJV) says, "A wise man is strong, yes, a man of knowledge increases strength."

As you grow in godly knowledge, you increase in strength. Just knowing these things increases your strength. Knowing that tough times don't last increases your strength. Knowing that you'll never face more than you can bear increases your strength.

The ultimate issue is not that you have problems. We all have problems. Through your relationship with the Lord you know Someone Who can do something about those problems. There is nothing that God cannot do, cannot help, and cannot fix. You've got to have sustained right thinking, which is thinking in line with the Word of God. The problem is not the issue; strength is the issue.

Stop telling God about your big problems. Start telling your problems about your big God. Cowboy up! No matter what you're facing, it won't take you out permanently and it won't last forever. Lean on the Lord and He will give you more and more grace. He'll also give you wisdom to navigate through your tough times.

There's no way you can realistically identify every potential problem that might come along. The key is finding an approach that will enable you to overcome the challenges, pressure, adversity and tough times. That's what I want to share with you in this book. Just like a soldier going into battle, you need the proper equipment and preparation. As you get informed and equipped, find strength and make right decisions, you'll be headed in the right direction. Then you can deal with the tough times when they come along and make sure they don't linger. ⌒

CHAPTER 2

STRENGTH IS THE ISSUE

When he was about five or six, my youngest son, Gabriel, had a doctor's appointment for allergy testing, which required having blood drawn.

"Buddy," I told him, "I need you to be brave today because the nurse is going to take some blood out of your arm. After that, I'll get you a surprise."

I have to admit, when I was a kid, I used to fake being sick just to get a Matchbox car. That was my favorite surprise. (I still have my Matchbox cars, thank you very much.)

Gabriel was nervous because this testing was all new to him. He was concerned about the size of the needle and whether or not it would hurt. He was apprehensive because the whole situation was foreign to him; he just didn't know what to expect. When they finally called his name and we went back to the examining room, he was as brave as he could be, watching the nurse do what she had to do. After the blood was drawn and the Band-Aid® was in place, he looked at me and said, "Dad, that wasn't so bad after all."

I realized later we're often just like Gabriel and that visit to the doctor. We don't know what's going to happen next, so we start to get ourselves worked up and nervous. We listen to the news, we hear the stock market reports, we talk to friends, and we can easily find ourselves in a negative spiral imagining the worst. If we just stop and think, we'll remember that we've been through tough times in the past and somehow, through the grace of God, we made it through.

GAINING STRENGTH

How successfully — or miserably — we make it through challenges in life depends in part on what we know. The prophet Hosea said, "My people are destroyed for lack of knowledge." This indicates that if they had knowledge, they probably wouldn't be destroyed.

It's been said, *"The ignorance of the oppressed is the strength of the oppressor."*

In John 8:32 (NKJV), Jesus said, *"And you shall know the truth, and the truth shall make you free."* This is why it's so important that we gain knowledge.

Proverbs 24:5 (NKJV) says, "A wise man is strong, yes, a man of knowledge increases strength." As you'll soon discover, strength is the issue.

Let's look at the apostle Paul. He was a danger to the religious leaders and officials of his day, so they wanted him off the streets. They had him arrested and put on trial. As the accused, Paul faced a series of hearings. It was a lengthy, emotionally exhausting process.

In 2 Timothy 4:16-17 (NKJV), Paul says, "At my first defense no one stood with me, but all forsook me. May it not be charged against them. But the Lord stood with me and strengthened me, so that the message might be preached fully through me, and that all the Gentiles might hear. Also I was delivered out of the mouth of the lion."

Paul's reference to the "mouth of the lion" was because he faced certain death. He was all alone. His friends, the people he counted on and hoped would be there to support him, bailed on him. But here's the most important thing: the Lord stood with him and Paul knew that beyond any shadow of a doubt.

Keep in mind, this was decades after Jesus was crucified, buried and rose from the dead. The Lord Himself didn't physically walk into that courtroom and stand beside Paul, but Paul felt His presence just as surely as if He had been there in the flesh. The resurrection power and presence of the Lord showed up and made the difference. We need to realize that the same power and presence are available for us today.

Paul said, "The Lord stood with me and strengthened me"… and notice what he said next… "so that the message might be preached fully through me, and that all the Gentiles might hear."

Paul never forgot his purpose, even under the strain of trial and abandonment by his friends.

Sometimes we get so focused on our problems, that we forget our purpose. Notice this… the reason the Lord stood with Paul and strengthened him was for his purpose. It wasn't just so Paul would feel better. Granted, Paul certainly felt better because the Lord strengthened him and helped him, but that was because Paul was focused on his purpose.

We, too, must be purpose-minded rather than just focused on our discomforts. If the only reason we want the Lord to help and strengthen us is so we feel better, then we are mere babies. Everything is big for a baby. Instead of focusing on getting comfort and relief so we feel better, we should be focused on a purpose that is greater than our current discomfort.

I believe some of you are to be paymasters for the Kingdom of God to help fund ministries and missions and get things done for the Kingdom. We're here on this earth, at this specific time, to make an impact and to make a difference in people's lives. You'll find that the Lord will come and stand with you and strengthen you, so that you can fulfill your purpose. The more purpose-minded you are, the more you will experience the strength of God helping you during tough times.

Consider this: the Lord did not remove Paul from the trial, and He did not remove the trial from Paul. Instead, He came and *joined with* Paul right where he was in the middle of that situation. He strengthened him and encouraged him, so that Paul could bear up under it and eventually walk away from it.

In 2 Timothy 4:18 (NKJV), Paul says, "And the Lord will deliver me from every evil work and preserve me for His heavenly kingdom. To Him be glory forever and ever. Amen!"

You need to realize God WILL deliver you. That is why I can say with confidence, "tough times don't last!" The Bible is all about God's deliverance. God is forever coming in to do two things: rescue and preserve. This is what God does. That's His whole method of operation. He rescues you and preserves you. He's all about making you whole, snatching you out, fixing you up and causing you to be useful for others.

God rescues you, preserves you and helps you. How does He do this? He strengthens you. Remember, **strength is the issue.**

We often beg God to get us out of tough situations instead of asking Him for strength so we can endure. God strengthens us with his grace. A lot of people think of "grace" as something you say when you sit down to eat, but that's not really what grace is about. That's just a term we have adopted to thank God for our food and for His faithfulness.

As John Newton wrote in his powerful song, "Amazing Grace," it's grace that got us this far, and grace will get us home. Grace is the issue, because God's grace helps and strengthens us.

Throughout the New Testament we find mention of the word grace. In the Amplified Bible, grace is referred to as "spiritual favors and spiritual strength." In 2 Timothy 2:1 (AMP), Paul is writing to Timothy and says, "So you, my son, be strong (strengthened inwardly) in the grace (spiritual blessing) that is [to be found only] in Christ Jesus."

Here's the deal. If we're going to be strong, it's only by *His grace*. We already know grace gives us strength, but where it strengthens us is very, very important. Grace brings inner strength... which is right where we need it. We've got to have grace on the inside. When you hear bad news, where do you feel it the most? On the inside. The cloud starts on the inside. That's why we desperately need God's grace to make us strong in the inner man.

Paul assured Timothy that grace is only to be found through trust in Jesus Christ. That's still the case today. It's not found online or through any other source. Jesus Christ is the "exclusive distributor," the only Source, for the grace that strengthens on the inside.

We must have this grace and strength; we cannot survive without it. If we do not have His grace, which is His strength, EVERYTHING is a problem. If we have the grace, we have the strength. Without His grace, without His strength, we are living "grace-less." Think about it. We cannot survive, let alone truly succeed, without grace. We can try to make good decisions, we can

The very real, very personal ministry of the Holy Spirit is to give you strength when you need it.

make vows and promises to change and improve. We can be sincere, determined, even desperate, but without God's grace strengthening us on the inside, we're lost.

A CLOSER LOOK AT GRACE

Let's look more closely at grace. First of all, grace is the personal work of the Holy Spirit. Many believers are confused about what the Holy Spirit does, but His main job is to come in and strengthen you. He wants to be the Helper in your life. He literally delivers the grace you need when you need it. When you're not on church property, when you're out there living life, when you have to deal with stuff... it's the grace of God that comes to help in your time of need. The very real, very personal ministry of the Holy Spirit is to give you strength when you need strength.

Secondly, you need to know that His grace is sufficient. Another translation of 2 Corinthians 12:9 says that His grace "is enough." That means it's proportionate. The amazing grace that is found on the inside and is only found through trust in Christ Jesus is proportionate to whatever you're experiencing in life. If you've got a little problem, He'll give you grace sufficient for that problem. If you get hit with a huge problem, or more than one problem, He'll bring you the grace to get through that, too. His grace is sufficient. It's proportionate. It's enough.

Think about it this way. If there's a crack in your driveway with a little bit of grass growing through, you don't go order a bulldozer to dig it up. You just reach down and pull it up. You do what is proportionate for the task at hand. That's how God operates. He knows exactly how much grace you need to bring you through ANY situation. If more problems crop up, guess what? He'll see that you have more grace to get through.

God's grace is available. James 4:6 says, "He gives more and more grace to those humble enough to receive."

I'll get in that line!

I know that without His grace, His strength, none of us could make it. You might be facing a situation that you never expected. You may be telling yourself, "There's no way I can make it through this." On your own, that may be the case... but you aren't alone. You can and will make it through because Christ's grace is sufficient for whatever trial you're facing. He's promised that no matter what we are dealing with, His grace is enough. You may not even be able to fully explain it, but the grace of God strengthens you, bears you up, and somehow you make it through.

Grace doesn't alter or change the situation. Grace changes you. Circumstances can, and will, change. Everything may be pressing against you right now. Just stay plugged into God. Sometimes tough situations arise and it looks like they will take you down and out. Before long, they're behind you. You can look back and realize grace got you through, yet again. God's grace is your "one-stop-shop." It's what you need and it will carry you through.

God is able to deliver. He rescues and delivers! God alters things, halts things, and reverses things. My mission is to help God's people get equipped with His grace, which will strengthen us on the inside. No matter what is pressing us on the outside, we've got to be bigger on the inside, because that's where we feel it when the pressure is on.

HANDLING THE STRESS

When an engineer designs a massive structure, such as the Brooklyn Bridge or the Golden Gate Bridge, he must keep a number of things in mind. He has to take into account three loads, or stresses: the dead load, the live load, and the wind load.

The "dead load" is the weight of the bridge itself. The structure must be braced and strengthened so it can hold itself up before any other weight can be added. If you've ever worked with Lincoln Logs, or Legos®, you know you've got to be careful not to make them too top heavy, or the whole thing will fall.

The second stress the engineer must consider is the "live load," which is the weight of daily traffic, all the vehicles and people going back and forth. Not only does the bridge have to be strong enough to support itself, it must hold up all those people and all their baggage.

The third and final stress is the "wind load," or the pressure from storms, wind, rain, snow, and other weather-related events.

In order to be safe and useful, the bridge has to be strong enough to handle its own weight, the load of those who depend on it, and any storm that can rise against it. Our lives are much the same.

For starters, you must have enough strength to handle the "dead load," which is simply the load of you. You've got to have enough strength to support yourself — your thoughts and feelings about your past, present, and future. You need that strength on the inside to hold yourself up before you can deal with anything else in life. The sad thing is that many people lack the strength to hold up the dead load, so they endeavor to prop themselves up on drugs, alcohol, relationships, hobbies, habits, and all manner of other things. That's because they haven't tapped into the inner strength from God's grace that is more than enough.

Secondly, you have the "live load," which is daily living. The live load encompasses your family, your job, and your friends. It includes all the people you must deal with, all their baggage, all the projects and responsibilities you face in life. Bearing up under that load requires real strength. The strength that comes from the grace of God strengthens you on the inside and is more than enough. It's enough to hold you up and also to support the life you're called to live.

Thirdly, you have the "wind load," which covers all the storms, crises, tough times, and emergencies that will undoubtedly come into your life. When you're under pressure, you've got to have strength so you don't cave in. You never know when a storm will hit, so you must be strong.

Through God's grace, you have the strength to handle each of these loads. When you put your trust in Him, He strengthens you, He enables you, and He helps you to bear up under anything and everything.

In 2 Corinthians 12:9 (AMP), Paul is writing to the believers at Corinth about struggles he was facing. "But He said to me, 'My grace (My favor and loving kindness and mercy) is enough for you [sufficient against any danger and enables you to bear the trouble manfully]....'"

Isn't that awesome? We read in Isaiah 40:29 (NKJV), "He gives power to the weak, and to *those who have no might*, He increases strength."

In Philippians 4:12b-13 (AMP), Paul says, "I have learned in any and all circumstances the secret of facing every situation, whether well-fed or going hungry, having a sufficiency and enough to spare or going without and being in want."

And what is the secret?

Paul says in verse 13, "I have strength for all things in Christ Who empowers me [I am ready for anything, and equal to anything through Him Who infuses inner strength into me; I am self-sufficient in Christ's sufficiency]."

I am ready for anything. Wouldn't that be a good thing to be able to say?

In Habakkuk 3:17-19 (NKJV), the prophet echoes this same thought: "Though the fig tree may not blossom, nor fruit be on the vines; though the labor of the olive may fail; and the fields yield no food; though the flock may be cut off from the fold; and there be no herd in the stalls — yet I will rejoice in the Lord, I will joy in the God of my salvation. The Lord God is my strength; He will make my feet like deer's feet, and He will make me walk on my high hills."

Habakkuk was talking about dire times; things certainly didn't look good, but he knew where to find strength. He was convinced the Lord would carry him through.

Psalm 27:1b (NKJV) says, "The Lord is the strength of my life; of whom shall I be afraid?"

The Lord is our strength. This should be our banner and battle cry. His grace strengthens us on the inside. Once we have that inward strength from God, the rest is just details and a matter of time. On the other hand, if we don't have strength, this tells us there's a problem with our connection to God.

Everything else in life can waits its turn,

but we can't neglect this most vital relationship.

We've got to stay plugged into God!

If you put a piece of bread in the toaster and push down the lever, you expect a piece of toast to pop up… unless, of course, the toaster isn't plugged in. If that's the case, you can sit and wait all day, but you're never going to have toast. There's nothing wrong with your toaster, but it can't do its job when it's unplugged.

It's the same with us and our connection to God. No matter how frenzied and busy life gets, we must guard that connection. Everything else in life can wait its turn, but we can't neglect this most vital relationship. We've got to stay plugged into God! He's the God of all grace. He's rich in grace and mercy. He desires to give us the strength to help. If we try operating without grace, everything and everyone ends up bugging us. But when we connect with grace, it's a different story.

All of us face problems. Without grace, those problems will pile up and become mountains. But remember… problems aren't the issue. Strength is the issue and our strength comes from the Lord, as long as we stay plugged in and connected to Him. He may not take the problems away or whisk you out of the situation, but I'll tell you what He'll do. He will join you, give you strength and save you from the mouth of the lion. He'll rescue and preserve you.

Romans 16:20 (NKJV) tells us, "And the God of peace will crush Satan under your feet shortly. The grace of our Lord Jesus Christ be with you."

This is such an incredible Scripture and one of my favorites in the entire Bible. Paul wrote this to encourage the believers then and it encourages us today. "The God of peace will crush Satan..." refers to the future, so we know the victory is coming. "The grace of our Lord Jesus Christ be with you" refers to the present.

He's with us. Even in tough times, we can be assured of this amazing truth: He's standing with us and His all-sufficient, unending grace strengthens us. Tough times don't last, but by God's grace, *you will last.* ⌣

CHAPTER 3

DON'T CARRY YOUR CARES

If we've learned anything, it's that we need to be strong to make it through tough times, and we've discovered where to find that strength.

Psalm 18:1b (NKJV) says, "I will love You, O Lord, my strength. The Lord is my rock, my fortress and my deliverer; my God, my strength in Whom I will trust; my shield and the horn of my salvation, my stronghold."

One of my favorite verses is Psalm 27:1 (NKJV), which says, "The Lord is my light and my salvation; whom shall I fear? The Lord is the strength of my life; of whom shall I be afraid?"

In Psalm 28:6-7, we read: "Blessed be the Lord, because He has heard the voice of my supplications. The Lord is my strength and my shield; my heart trusted in Him, and I am helped; therefore my heart greatly rejoices, and with my song I will praise Him."

These Scriptures encourage us to cry out to God when we're going through trials. Many times we have not, because we ask not.

In Habakkuk 3:19 (NKJV), the prophet declared, "The Lord God is my strength!"

In Philippians 4:13 (NKJV), the apostle Paul wrote, "I can do all things through Christ Who strengthens me."

DEALING WITH WEAKNESS

We know that strength is the issue, not the problems we face. Yet, too often, we find ourselves weak and struggling, and the tough times seem even tougher. Why? If God is our source, a never-ending supply of grace and strength, then why do we end up weak? If God is always there to provide sufficient grace in the situation we're facing, why do we sometimes lack the strength we so desperately need?

The answer isn't pretty, but it's simple: He gives us strength, and we lose it. We give it away.

This reminds me of being a kid at the county fair. When I was growing up, my folks would give me five bucks. That won't even get you in the gate today, but back then it was enough to get in, go on rides, and eat some of that fair food. Those were the days! I'd always end up at that booth with the air-powered BB gun where you were supposed to shoot out the star and you could win a motorhome or something extravagant. I loved that game, but I never won. I realized later there was no way I could win because the sights were off on the gun. I'd keep playing, determined to win, and sooner or later, I was out of money and hungry. I still had hours to go, but I'd spent everything I'd been given.

We do the same thing with the strength the Lord gives us. He gives us all we need, but we spend it and give it away. Then we end up weak and that's when we get in trouble.

It's easy to say, "Well, just stop doing that." But first, we need to understand that there are things that increase our strength and there are things that decrease our strength. Some of these things should be obvious. Church, for example, increases our strength, because church days affect the rest of our days. There are programs you watch on TV and books you read that increase strength; there are plenty of others that take away strength. You can hang out with some people who build you up and increase your strength. With other people you can actually feel your strength drain away when you're around them. We must be on guard because strength is what we need.

Let's go back to the Old Testament in Judges chapters 14–16 and look at Samson. He had incredible strength that came directly from the Lord. It wasn't that Samson was a massive specimen of a man. People wouldn't have been so perplexed about his great strength if he was a hulk of a guy. They kept trying to find the secret of his strength, because he was an average man who did astounding things. On more than one occasion, his enemies tied him up with new rope and he broke free as if those ropes were mere threads. Another time he killed one thousand men with the jawbone of a donkey.

People kept asking, "What is it about this guy? How does he do this?" The truth was that Samson only had his amazing strength when the spirit of the Lord came upon him.

Eventually, Samson got involved with the wrong people and in wrong activities. He was lulled into carelessness and gave away the secret of his strength. We've got to be careful of doing the same thing. We have to be aware and keep our attention focused on God so we don't become diverted and allow the strength He so freely gives us to drain away.

Your strength is valuable; you have to guard it. You can't surf the Internet mindlessly. You can't sit in front of the TV for hours watching anything that comes on. You need to use discretion about who you hang out with, what you're talking about, and what you're doing. If you aren't careful, you will compromise your strength. You'll lose strength, and remember... strength is the issue. Don't give away your strength!

The book of Proverbs is full of wisdom. I encourage everyone to read a Proverb every day; there are 31 chapters, so you can read a new Proverb every day of the month and then start over.

In Proverbs 5 (NKJV), we read the account of an immoral woman. Proverbs 5:3 says, "For the lips of an immoral woman drip honey, and her mouth is smoother than oil."

The Proverbs were originally written in Hebrew by King Solomon. If you look up this verse in the Hebrew language, the phrase "immoral woman" actually means "to turn aside." You were probably expecting "floozy" or "tramp," but the literal translation is "to turn aside."

This immoral woman is not a real person, but is figurative. She is symbolic and refers to anything that causes you to turn aside and step off the path.

In the beginning, the description appears to be pleasurable. Her mouth drips honey and is smoother than oil. Proverbs 7 gives a similar account of an immoral woman, and again, the initial description is enticing and intriguing. Read on, however, and you'll find the story ends in pain, loss, destruction and regret.

Proverbs 5:4 (NKJV) reads, "But in the end she is bitter as wormwood, sharp as a two-edged sword." Wormwood is a reference to poison... bitterness and poison. The two-edged sword cuts you up... slices and dices and makes julienne fries out of your life.

The Message Bible puts it this way: "But it won't be long before she's gravel in your mouth, a pain in your gut, a wound in your heart."

Let me put it a different way. There are certain kinds of fast food that every now and then, I just start craving. You know what it's like... you're driving by and you can almost taste it. Your windows are up, but you can smell it. You pull in and order five of them! You wolf them down and they taste so good... but before you get to the next red light, it feels like you have three pairs of wet socks wadded up in your stomach. You're asking yourself, "Why did I do that?" You go home and your wife says, "You don't look so good." And you say, "Don't even ask... and I'm not hungry!"

Each one of us knows what that "immoral woman" represents in our own lives. You recognize the things that pull at you. There are many things that tug on us in different ways. They distract us and entice us to turn aside and step off the path. What seems pleasurable at the start becomes gravel in your mouth, a pain in your gut, and a wound in your heart.

Proverbs 5:8 reads, "Remove your way far from her, and do not go near the door of her house...."

I have a little principle for that: the long way is better than the wrong way. Don't go near her house; don't even look down her road. Whatever "she" is for you, whatever it is that pulls at you, tries to turn you aside, you need to take the long way rather than the wrong way.

Proverbs 5:9 (NKJV) continues, "Lest you give your honor to others, and your years to the cruel one."

If you continue down that road, you're going to give it all away… and it won't be to charity. You'll give away your strength, your honor, your wealth, your name, and all that you worked for. You will give it away and end up in ruin.

Skip down to verses 12 and 13, which essentially say, "I should have listened. I should have listened to my mentors, my teachers, my pastor, my friends, my wise friends… I should have listened. Instead I find myself on the verge of total ruin in the midst of the congregation."

Church goers and followers of Jesus are not exempt from wandering off the path. Things come along in life and tempt you to turn off the path. They

We lose our strength when we're overly focused on the cares of life. Pressure, anxiety, cares … everyone has them. The secret is to do something other than carry them.

may look good in the beginning, but ultimately they will drain away your strength and take away your good name, your honor, your wealth, all that you worked for, and bring you to a place of ruin. Stay on the path. Do not give away your strength!

HANDLING OUR CARES

There are two major ways we give away our strength. Number one: the cares of life. We lose our strength when we're overly focused on the cares of life. Pressure, anxiety, cares… everyone has them. The secret is to do something other than carry them.

News flash! You and I are not equipped to carry the cares of life. We think we're pretty smart, we're tough, and have a high pain tolerance. But, my friend, you are not equipped to carry cares. That was never God's intention for you.

When you shoulder your own cares and burdens, there is an immediate physiological response. It affects your blood pressure, your respiration and heart rate. It causes the release of stomach acids and affects your digestion. Your whole body is negatively impacted when you try to carry your cares. It's like trying to tow an enormous trailer behind a little tiny car... it's just not up to the task.

You are much the same as that little car struggling to budge an overloaded trailer. This is not meant to hurt your pride, but rather to set you free. You simply aren't able to handle the load.

The cares of this life weigh us down, sap our strength, choke our faith, blur our vision, hijack our emotions, and take over our thought life. We're not meant to carry those cares, yet, what do we do? We constantly carry cares!

We all know what happens when you suddenly get bad news. You can literally feel your strength leaving. It's almost instantaneous. That's the very moment when you need to plug the drain and get plugged back into the source of your strength.

The cares of life aren't going away. So how do we handle them if we aren't equipped to carry them? The Bible gives us the solution: cast your cares.

1 Peter 5:7-8 (AMP) says: "Casting the whole of your care [all your anxieties, all your worries, all your concerns, once and for all] on Him, for He cares for you affectionately and cares about you watchfully. Be well balanced (temperate, sober of mind), be vigilant and cautious at all times; for that enemy of yours, the devil, roams around like a lion roaring [in fierce hunger], seeking someone to seize upon and devour."

Can I give you some news? The devil is looking for lunch! Like a hungry lion on the prowl, he's not looking to take down the whole herd at once. No, he looks for the one that falls behind. He seeks out the weak one, the one who turns aside and is struggling on his own. There's a scent about the weakened one who is carrying cares, and the devil seeks that one out to devour. You don't want to be the devil's snack. You've got to cast those cares.

In the New Testament, "casting" actually means "to throw upon." Notice this is not just "to throw" but "to throw UPON." This means you're casting those cares somewhere... where? On the Lord. You throw them off yourself and on the Lord.

The root of that word refers to something done suddenly, as in "to fling" or "to hurl." Think of how you would react if you were walking in the woods and a spider drops on your neck. There's nothing slow or casual about your reaction; you FLING that spider off! If you accidentally step in an ant bed, you don't just stand there and let them crawl up your legs. No, you start dancing to get those ants off of you.

That's how we're supposed to react to our cares. Psalm 37:5 (AMP) says: "Commit your way to the Lord [roll and repose each care of your load on Him]; trust (lean on, rely on, and be confident) also in Him and He will bring it to pass."

Psalm 55:22 (AMP) reads: "Cast your burden on the Lord [releasing the weight of it] and He will sustain you; He will never allow the [consistently] righteous to be moved (made to slip, fall, or fail)."

We need to do whatever it takes to get rid of our cares. That may mean singing, shouting, praying, reading, running, changing the channel or asking somebody for help, but do what you have to do to get out from under that load of cares.

Many of you have been camping and discovered a bug near your sleeping bag, or maybe even IN your sleeping bag. You quickly get rid of it, but the thought of that bug stays with you. Even though you know it's gone, you can't help but think about it. If you let yourself, you can still feel it, and that's not a good feeling. Before you know it, you're looking around for more bugs.

This is precisely the nature of cares. There are times when you deal with something troubling and even after it's over, you can still feel it weighing on you. Cares *compress* you; they *depress* you, which means "to press down." You've dealt with the issue, but you continue to feel that depression. What's going on? Probably nothing, but here's what you need to do: shower in the Holy Spirit! Get rid of the residue of those cares. Declare your freedom: "I'm free from that; there's nothing weighing on me. I'm happy, I'm well, don't come near me!"

DON'T CARRY THE BURDEN

There's a danger in continually carrying cares. When you're weighed down, you can easily tip over. When you're carrying a load that you're not equipped to carry, it's easy to knock you over, to tip you over, and to offend you.

Notice that last one... to offend you. **Holding onto an offense is the second major way we lose strength.**

We routinely hear about incidents of road rage in the news. However annoying the traffic situation, road rage usually has little to do with what's going on at the moment. It's more about what happened to you earlier in the

"Great peace have they who love Your law;

nothing shall offend them

or make them stumble."

day, the week, or even earlier in your life. You're mad about something else and your fuse is short because you're carrying cares, which makes you easily offended.

Offense diverts your attention, eats at your joy, and drains your strength. We often feel justified about being offended, because we've been wronged. We're mad at a person, we're mad at the system... we're just plain mad. But even when we feel we have a "right" to be upset, that feeling of offense drains our joy and strength. The next thing we know, we're weak because we're carrying those offenses and cares.

Remember this: anger is a secondary emotion. When you're strong, things that would otherwise offend you don't matter. When you're clear-minded, all those things that threaten to tip you over just can't bring you down.

Proverbs 19:11 (NKJV) says, "The discretion of a man makes him slow to anger, and his glory is to overlook a transgression." A transgression is another word for an offense.

Psalm 119:165 (AMP) says, "Great peace have they who love Your law;

nothing shall offend them or make them stumble."

If you love His law, you'll grow in strength and you won't give that strength away by being easily offended.

The New Testament word for offense is the Greek word "skandalon," which means a "bait stick, a trap stick, or a snare." In Africa, it's said that monkey hunters will set up a trap, or cage, and place a bait stick, or skandalon, in the middle of it. If the skandalon is tripped, the cage door will close. The monkey is usually too smart to fall for this and won't enter the cage. Instead, he'll go around to the back of the trap and reach his arm through the bars to grab the skandalon. Once his fist closes over the bait, he's too stubborn to let go. When the hunter shows up, he can easily capture or kill the monkey because the animal — even though he isn't actually in the trap — is caught by his own stubbornness, his refusal to let go.

Don't be a monkey! Is holding onto an offense worth going into captivity? Is it worth being destroyed? Holding onto an offense is just like that stubborn monkey clinging to the bait stick when he could walk away and be free.

LET IT GO! When you let go of offense and cast your cares on the Lord, your strength will return.

We've seen how we lose and decrease strength. So how do we gain and increase that vital strength?

I came across a wise Serbian proverb: "Solitude is full of God." There's the answer to increasing your strength.

Here is another powerful statement by Dallas Willard, a theologian, philosopher and author of *The Spirit of the Disciplines: Understanding How God Changes Lives*. "It is solitude, and solitude alone, that opens the possibility of a radical relationship to God that can withstand all external events up to and beyond death."

Solitude is full of God, and time alone with Him is the quickest way to find strength. Cast your cares and let go of offense. The Lord is the strength of your life. Call on Him, spend solitary time with Him, walk with Him, turn your focus on Him... and He will supply all the strength you need. ✑

CHAPTER 4

IT'S ALL ABOUT RELATIONSHIP

When we're in the midst of tough times, often our focus is purely on our escape. We don't want to "deal" with it and we don't want to cope; we just want those difficult circumstances to go away.

Yet, in 2 Peter 1:2-4 (NKJV) we read, "Grace and peace be multiplied to you in the knowledge of God and of Jesus our Lord, as His divine power has given to us all things that pertain to life and godliness, through the knowledge of Him who called us by glory and virtue, by which have been given to us exceedingly great and precious promises, that through these you may be partakers of the divine nature...."

When Peter is talking about grace and peace being multiplied, he isn't referring to the perfect setting of heaven. Notice the rest of that sentence. Grace and peace are multiplied to us *in the knowledge of God and Jesus our Lord.* Peter goes on to say that God's divine power has given us everything we need for life and godliness *through the knowledge of Him.*

Peter makes it clear that everything we need in this life — no matter how tough times may be — is available through knowing God. Not only does this knowledge of God provide what we need, it also multiplies grace and peace.

GETTING TO KNOW GOD

Whether we realize it or not, we each have a hunger in our hearts, and that hunger is for:

1. Intimacy with God
2. Intimacy with others
3. Self-worth

There's a reason intimacy with God is number one on that list, and that's because everything is connected to your relationship with God. If everything we need comes through intimate — close and personal — knowledge of God, that means if we don't have this kind of relationship with Him, we'll miss out. Why? Certainly, not because God withholds or draws back, but because He's designed it so that we need to come to Him to receive His promises.

If this is the case, a relationship with God must be our first priority, our greatest goal. But what exactly does it mean to "know" God?

Talking to God through prayer is one way of creating a relationship with Him, but if we're honest, most of us will admit we're usually asking God for something when we pray. We may want Him to fix something, to change something (or someone), to intervene or turn things around. There is nothing wrong with this. God wants to do work in our lives. He is willing, able, and pleased when we bring our requests to Him, rather than try to handle the situation on our own.

Yet, too often our prayer time is only about our requests, and then we go on about our day. God is not a supernatural vending machine. We need to consider that God may have something to "say" to us. If we treated our human friendships the way we treat our relationship with God, we probably wouldn't have many friends left. We have one mouth and two ears. This is a clue. We should be doing more listening than talking.

Listening is vital to communication, communication is vital to intimacy, and intimacy with God is vital to our lives. Many times, we find ourselves in tough situations that could have been avoided if only we'd listened to God earlier.

Real communication involves talking AND listening; both are vital for true intimacy. We actually do God — and ourselves — a disservice by not allowing Him to speak into our lives. Any healthy relationship is a two-way street; both parties need to have the opportunity to share their hearts.

So if God knows the best thing to do, the best way to handle any circumstance, wouldn't it be wise to invite Him to speak to you?

God wants to share His heart with you. Think about it. He is all powerful and all knowing; if anybody knows what to do in tough times, it's God! So if God knows the best thing to do, the best way to handle any circumstance, wouldn't it be wise to invite Him to speak to you?

As you start paying attention and listening to God, your Christianity becomes "relational." On the other hand, if you're too busy talking to God and never stop to listen to what He has to say, your faith will erode into ritual, routine and religion. Religion is all based on man's efforts. Plenty of people have religion, but have no real relationship with God.

I believe there are times in life when we have serious needs — sometimes we're even in crisis — and God wants to say something to us. He may not change things instantly, but simply by hearing Him, we find what we need in that situation.

You may be thinking, *but how can God talk to me?* Our greatest example is none other than Jesus Christ Himself.

No one understood the need for communication with God as clearly or practiced this better than Jesus. He made it a priority — a daily habit — to spend time alone with the Father.

In Mark 1:32-33 (NKJV)), we read "… at evening, when the sun had set, they brought to Him all who were sick and those who were demon possessed. And the whole city was gathered together at the door. Then He healed many who were sick with various diseases, and cast out many demons...."

Jesus was busy helping people all day and well into the night. He had to be exhausted, but He didn't sleep in the next morning.

Verses 35 and 36 continue: "Now in the morning, having risen a long while before daylight, He went out and departed to a solitary place; and there He prayed. And Simon and those who were with Him searched for Him. When they found Him, they said to Him, 'Everyone is looking for You.'"

Simon's implication was clear: "We've got a lot to do, so what are You doing out here?"

But Jesus knew something they hadn't yet grasped. He knew He couldn't fulfill His mission if He didn't make it a priority to spend time with His Father. Everything depended on that.

In Mark 6:45-46, Jesus had spent the day teaching and miraculously fed the crowd of thousands with just five loaves of bread and two fishes. After the multitude went home and He sent the disciplines on to the next town, Jesus departed to the mountain to pray.

We read in Luke 5:15-16 (NKJV), "However, the report went around concerning Him all the more; and great multitudes came together to hear, and to be healed by Him of their infirmities. So He Himself often withdrew into the wilderness and prayed."

Jesus knew His priorities. He went from place of prayer to place of prayer, doing miracles and ministering to people in between. We tend to do everything else and try to cram a little bit of prayer in between.

Even though Jesus came to earth for the express purpose of doing God's will, He had to maintain a relationship with His Father in order to accomplish this. That meant valuing and prioritizing time with God over the needs of the people, over his friends and family... over everything else. All the life-changing things Jesus did came out of His time alone with the Father. If it worked for Jesus, it will work for us.

Jesus basically said, "I came to do the will of the Father, and if I don't know it, I can't do it."

Read the Gospels and study the pattern of His ministry; you'll see that He constantly checked in with the Father. In essence, Jesus was saying, "*I only do what I see my Father doing. I only say what I hear my Father say. The things that I am doing are what I see my Father doing.*"

BUILDING A RELATIONSHIP

To build a real relationship with God, you need to spend time alone, just you and God. There's no substitute.

Spending time alone with God does not make Him love you more than He already does. You don't earn special spiritual reward bonus points. It simply makes it easier for God to communicate with you.

For me, the best time to do this is first thing in the morning. The day is fresh, the chalkboard is clean. I haven't been pressed, compressed or depressed. If late at night works best for you, that's fine, but whenever you set time aside for God, it needs to be a priority.

I would rather start my day right rather than try to salvage my day later. For that reason, I like the concept of "First and Final 15," which means spending the first 15 minutes of the day, in the morning, with God, and the last 15 minutes before going to sleep. You may start with this, but don't be surprised to find the time expand because you want to spend more time with your Father.

There are several steps you can take to build a solid relationship with God. There is no guaranteed method or set of rules, but these practices have been fruitful in my own life.

1. Start with your heart.

When you approach your time with God, invest your whole heart. *Your heart cannot be in what your mind is not on.* Do whatever it takes to put your mind on what you're doing so you can put your heart into it.

Jeremiah 29:13-14 (NKJV) says, "'And you will seek Me and find Me, when you search for Me with all your heart. I will be found by you,' says the Lord...."

In Matthew 15:8-9 (NKJV), Jesus quotes the Prophet Isaiah: "*These people draw near to Me with their mouth and honor Me with their lips. But their heart is far from Me and in vain they worship Me....*"

Proverbs 23:26 (NKJV), says, "My son, give Me your heart, and let your eyes observe My ways."

Clearly, God wants our hearts involved as we seek after Him.

2. Set a time and find a place.

We live in hectic times. Everyone seems to be busy and the number one enemy of intimacy is busyness. The number two enemy is laziness. Every relationship must be maintained if you want it to last. It takes time and energy to build and maintain any relationship, and this applies to your relationship with God.

We need to use the Bible as a tool, because that's exactly what it is.

The Bible is the number one selling book of all time,

but it's not just for the coffee table.

You must commit to a time and place to seek Him. True, you can pray any time and any place. But once you start making it a habit to set aside a specific time in a particular place, it will be easier to hear from God.

I encourage you to set apart a place that you use only for spending time with God. It may be a chair in your study or bedroom, a rocker on your porch, or a corner of the guest room. It just needs to be a place that you always associate with your quest for God. One important thing to remember is that it is very hard to pray or read in the sleep position!

3. Read and write.

When I'm spending time with God, I don't want to just read the Bible. I want it to "speak" to me because I need to hear from God, and He reveals Himself through His Word. We need to learn to use the Bible as a tool because that's exactly what it is. The Bible is the number one selling book of all time, but it's not just for the coffee table.

Many times we're asking God for direction, for help, when all along the answers are right there. We're begging God to "say something" when He's already said so much.

Yes, God can speak in a dream or give someone a vision, but the number one way God speaks is through Scripture.

Christians today are fortunate in that we can read and study the Bible in many different ways. It's available online, on television, on CD, in print, on tape, in church... even on your smart phone!

All through Psalm 119, King David talks about how much he loves God's Word. At the time he wrote the Psalms, and specifically Psalm 119, history tells us that he probably only had exposure to about seven books of the Bible. He had access to far less Scripture than we do today, but David still found intimacy with the Father through the written Word.

In Psalm 119:97 (AMP), David says, "Oh, how I love Your law! It is my meditation all the day."

Psalm 119:102 (AMP) says, "I have not turned aside from Your ordinances, for You Yourself have taught me."

King David realized he wasn't just reading a book. He knew God Almighty was teaching him and speaking to him directly. David gained three things from the written Word: wisdom, insight, and understanding. We can expect to get the same.

I encourage you, as you read your Bible, to stop and think. Ask yourself what a particular verse or section means to you. Why is it here? What should you do about it? How can you remember it? Keep a journal or notebook so that when you get a thought on a verse, you can write it down and study it further.

Here's a simple prayer you can pray asking God to help you get more out of your time with Him: "Heavenly Father, let the light of Your Word shine down into the dark places of my heart. Let the promises of Your Word encourage my soul. Let the truth of Your Word reshape my attitudes. And let the wisdom of Your Word guide my decisions."

4. Pray.

Much of the time Jesus spent with the Father, He spent in prayer. Jesus knew the Word and studied the Word. In fact, Jesus *was* the Word, yet He still spent a great deal of time in prayer.

One of the biggest problems Christians have with praying is that they don't! God wants us to talk to Him and prayer is how we do that. It doesn't need to be fancy or dramatic; just talk to Him like you'd talk to a friend.

Here's a helpful acronym to get you started: ACTS. Your prayer life can be much richer and more effective if you simply think of this as a guideline.

A = Adoration

C = Confession

T = Thanksgiving

S = Supplication

Adoration and respect for God should be the launching point of our prayers. Declare that He is awesome; tell Him you love Him. Think of who He is and all He's done.

Psalm 103:1-2 (AMP) says, "Bless (affectionately, gratefully praise) the Lord, O my soul; and all that is [deepest] within me, bless His holy name! Bless (affectionately, gratefully praise) the Lord, O my soul, and forget not [one of] all His benefits."

Confession means to admit or acknowledge something. As you approach a Holy God, you may be aware of some things in your life that need forgiveness. Acknowledge and admit this, then confess it to God. Keep short accounts with God. Don't wait until the next day to ask for forgiveness. As soon as you are aware, get it right with God and, if necessary, get it right with man.

1 John 1:9 (NKJV) says, "If we confess our sins, He is faithful and just to forgive us our sins and to cleanse us from all unrighteousness."

Thanksgiving is about gratitude and appreciation.

Ephesians 5:20 (AMP) says, "At all times and for everything giving thanks in the name of our Lord Jesus Christ to God the Father."

We are to come with thanksgiving to the Lord for ALL things, yet let's face it, there are always things in life we aren't happy about. Are we really supposed to be thankful for those things?

If you do a little word study, you'll find that the Greek word "for" in this verse is actually the word "huper," which means "over, above, and beyond." When you understand the true definition of that single word, it adds depth to

God wants us to talk to Him and prayer is how we do that.

It doesn't need to be fancy or dramatic;

just talk to Him like you'd talk to a friend.

the entire verse. The apostle Paul was saying we should thank God OVER, ABOVE and BEYOND whatever is happening in our lives. This makes a lot more sense than thanking God for the flat tire you had on the way home from work!

1 Thessalonians 5:18 (AMP) says, "Thank [God] in everything [no matter what the circumstances may be, be thankful and give thanks]...."

No matter what is going on in your life, you can still thank God because, bottom line, you have much to be thankful for. I believe a major portion of our prayer time should be devoted to thanking God. Don't just think your thanks; speak it!

Supplication means to ask, to request, with definite petition. Come to God and tell Him what's on your heart. Ask Him to work. Ask Him what you should do. Make specific requests and expect an answer.

James 4:2b (AMP) tells us, "You do not have because you do not ask."

In Matthew 7:7-8 (AMP), Jesus says, *"Keep on asking and it will be given you; keep on seeking and you will find; keep on knocking [reverently] and [the door] will be opened to you. For everyone who keeps on asking receives; and he who keeps on seeking finds; and to him who keeps on knocking, [the door] will be opened."*

These verses make it very clear that we are to bring specific requests to God. Don't be vague! Tell Him your concerns, your needs. It's not that He doesn't already know, but He wants you to speak these things, to lay them out before Him.

"God will do nothing on earth except in answer to believing prayer," noted John Wesley, the 1700's Christian theologian who helped establish the Methodist church.

God is waiting to act in our lives, but we need to ask Him!

Philippians 4:6(AMP) reads, "Do not fret or have any anxiety about anything, but in every circumstance and in everything, by prayer and petition (definite requests), with thanksgiving, continue to make your wants known to God."

GET GROUNDED

One of my favorite people and a great communicator is Andy Stanley, a pastor in Georgia. In one of his messages, he made this statement: "If we could see things the way God sees things, we would be more inclined to do what God says."

The main reason we build a relationship with God is so we can begin to see things the way He sees them.

Isaiah 55:8-9 (AMP) says, "'For My thoughts are not your thoughts, neither are your ways My ways,' says the Lord. 'For as the heavens are higher than the earth, so are My ways higher than your ways and My thoughts higher than your thoughts.'"

Following Jesus and living the Christian life is more than just coming to church and getting goose bumps now and then. It's about learning God's ways so you can make wise decisions. Not all tough times can be avoided, but we can sidestep many troubles and lessen the impact of negative situations when we use wisdom. We can also get through difficult times without falling to pieces when we trust God and rely on our relationship with Him.

God will never make decisions for you, but when you have a relationship with Him, He'll guide you in making the right decisions on your own.

When you spend time with God and His Word, you gain wisdom, insight and understanding. This makes you less "tempt-able," because you can see through the enemy's lies, traps and tricks.

If you stop and think about it, there are three basic ways people learn in life:

1. Experience
2. Observation
3. Instruction

Experience is one of the most common — and most costly — ways to learn life's lessons, while observation allows you to learn from someone else's actions and/or mistakes. The highest form of learning is instruction, which can ultimately spare you enormous pain and negative consequences.

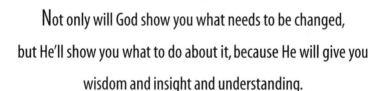

Not only will God show you what needs to be changed, but He'll show you what to do about it, because He will give you wisdom and insight and understanding.

Instruction is what most of God's Word is about. Psalm 119:105 (AMP) says, "Your Word is a lamp to my feet, and a light to my path."

Think about this literally. If you're walking in the woods at midnight, but you have a flashlight, you won't stumble or fall because light shines on the path ahead of you. That's precisely how God wants us to use His Word. As a loving Father, He desires to spare us from the painful consequences caused by the wrong turns and bad decisions we make in life. When you spend quiet time alone with God, reading the Bible and inviting Him to speak to you, you renew your mind and begin to shine the light of His wisdom on your life's path.

Time alone with God also enhances your sense of accountability. When you keep coming back to God and seeking His guidance, this allows Him to nudge your heart if there's something in your life that isn't right.

How will you recognize this "nudge" from your Heavenly Father? If you feel holy and precious discomfort, He's showing you something that needs to change. God Himself, the Creator of the Universe, is willing to speak to you, to patiently work with you one-on-one in loving and real life terms. This is the beginning of real, honest life change.

Hebrews 4:12 (NKJV) says, "For the Word of God is living and powerful, and sharper than any two-edged sword, piercing even to the division of soul and spirit, and of joints and marrow, and is a discerner of the thoughts and intents of the heart."

Only God's Word can get down to the place in your heart that is hidden from everyone else. It will show you why you are angry, why you are insecure, controlling, depressed, destructive, and fearful. It will reveal this if you will just give God your time, attention and a listening heart. Not only will God show you what needs to be changed, but He'll show you what to do about it, because He will give you wisdom and insight and understanding.

Perhaps you've never cultivated a personal relationship with God, or maybe you were closer to God in the past than you are now. Wherever you may be now, if there is distance between you and God, this allows room for other things to get in. When that happens, it's easy to seek other options for comfort and direction. You'll find yourself making unwise decisions that can ultimately lead to tough times.

Getting grounded in God must be the most important thing in your life, more important than work, more important than hobbies, schedules, and daily needs. It must be your number one priority. ⤸

CHAPTER 5

THE ESSENCE OF PROBLEM SOLVING

Your thoughts determine your direction. It's vital that you get your faith and your thoughts lined up with God's thoughts and words so that you can go where He intends for you to go.

We live in a world where there are tough times and challenges, but the Lord is the strength of our life. It's not just about us being tough and hanging on. Yes, we have a role to play; we are part of the equation. We need to have a little grit, a little fiber, about us, but at the same time, we are nothing without the Lord. On our own, we can do nothing.

God is our Source. He strengthens us on the inside. It's imperative that we lean on Him and declare this every day or many times throughout the day. The Lord is the strength of my life. Temptation, problems, adversity, pressure... whatever comes my way, the Lord is the strength of my life. That supernatural grace, that strength that He gives you on the inside, will get you through. His grace has brought us this far and His grace will take us all the way.

There are always two parts in the process of facing problems. There is God's part, which we cannot do, and there is our part, which God will not do. This is a very important combination and both roles are necessary if we want to come out on top of life's challenges. It is the grace-effort combo.

You always need to ask God to act and you should also ask Him to show you what to do. For every problem, you will find there is some kind of action God will show you to do. You can expect God to act, but you want His guidance, as well. You also need strength to move forward with whatever He shows you needs to be done. For some people, this seems too simple. They think it's immature to expect God to take care of things. Yes, God can take care of everything, but most of the time, He also wants us to do our part. I can't say this enough: *You can't do God's part and He won't do your part.*

I want you to grasp hold of this principle: *There is nothing in this life, nothing in this world, that is locked which God cannot unlock, or show you the key.* Whether He solves the problem miraculously or shows you what to do to solve it, either way, God is helping you.

Sometimes in life we run into situations where things are at an impasse. Statistics, polls, and the evening news say the situation is impossible. That's when we must remember that what is impossible with man is possible with God. We must remind ourselves there is nothing in the world that God cannot unlock. Get this truth: He can unlock it or He can show you the key. Either way, that situation, that problem, can get unlocked.

PROBLEM SOLVING

I want to share with you something I call "the essence of problem solving." To be honest, I've taken part of this from a message by Pastor A. R. Bernard, who pastors Christian Cultural Center in Brooklyn, New York, but don't worry, I've asked him for permission. He actually teaches "The Art of Problem Solving," but I've adapted a few things from part of his teaching and want to share with you the essence of problem solving. We need to understand that problem solving can be developed into an art form. We can literally become artists at solving problems.

First of all, you have to define the problem. In order to define the problem, you must recognize the definition of a problem. *A problem is a mismatch between what you have and what you want to have.* When you want one thing but you have something else, that, my friend, is a problem.

Let's say you go to your favorite restaurant. You've been thinking about a big, thick, juicy steak, broiled in butter, marbled perfectly, twelve ounces, and cooked just right. That's what you order and that's what you expect, but when the plate comes out, the meat looks like a broiled wallet... a little piece of beef jerky! What do you have? You have a problem... a mismatch between what you wanted and what you received.

Maybe you have to travel for business. Your flight arrives at the destination city and you follow the signs to baggage claim. After the conveyor belt

> # There is nothing in this life, nothing in this world, that is locked which God cannot unlock, or show you the key.

has gone around for the hundredth time, you realize your suitcase is not there. Or maybe it does show up, but it's obviously been opened because there's a sock or something hanging out, and you wonder what may be missing. You have a problem... a mismatch between what you have and what you want.

Some of the ladies can relate to this scenario. You find a photo in a magazine of a hairstyle you love, so you tear it out and take it to the beauty salon. You tell the stylist, "I want to look just like her." The stylist may roll her eyes behind your back, but hey, you're paying for it, so she goes to work. She shampoos, colors, cuts and works her magic. Then comes the final moment when she spins you around in the chair to face the mirror, but the hairstyle you now have isn't remotely what you expected. You have a problem... a mismatch between what you have and what you want.

Whether it's in your relationship, your family, your finances, your health, your career, or any other area... if you have a mismatch between what you want and what you have, there's a problem.

There's more to the process than simply defining the problem. Once you are sure about what you want, you need to understand what you have. You can't manage what you can't measure.

When they go out to eat, some people fail to tell the server exactly what they want. The meal comes out, but there's gravy on the chicken-fried steak and they don't eat gravy. Sometimes we start our own problems because we aren't clear about what we want — or don't want. We actually set ourselves up for a mismatch.

There are three things we must do:
- Clearly define what we want
- Understand what we have
- Decide what needs to be done

STEP BY STEP

When it comes to solving a problem, our first goal is to narrow the gap between what we have and what we want.

Einstein said, "You cannot solve a problem on the same level in which it was created."

The author of numerous books and founder of the Christian Men's Network, Dr. Edwin Louis Cole said, "Life is lived on levels and arrived at in stages."

I'm sure you're glad that you are not at the same level you were five or ten years ago. We should continually be going on to higher levels. From Einstein and Cole, we learn that in order to solve problems, we must go to another level. This means we have some work to do. We're going to have to pray, ask questions, gather information, and possibly even get someone else involved.

To solve a problem, you must go to a new level. You must admit there are things you don't know and go about gaining that knowledge. One thing is certain: you cannot be proud and be an effective problem solver. If you're proud, you think you know it all, you've got a problem. But pride will keep you from doing what it takes to go to that next level to find the solution. Guess what? You're never going to solve that problem. Things will just end up getting worse. Let's admit it: if we really knew it all, we wouldn't have problems.

Before you can solve anything, the **first thing you must do is admit your present condition.** It only gets worse if you try to deny it. Many times we have a problem, but we try to deny it, ignore it, hide it, or pretend it's not there.

One of the keys to successful problem solving is admitting your current condition. Otherwise, it will just pop up again… and again… and again.

My mom handled all the bills and correspondence in our family. She was sick for a number of years, and after she passed away, we found a box under her bed stuffed full of first, second and third notices on payments that were owed. She didn't want to deal with them, so she just tried to hide them away. In the end, we had to work with insurance agents to get everything sorted out and settled.

Jeremiah 6:14 in the Living Bible says, "You can't heal a wound by saying it's not there!"

Problems don't just go away if we ignore them. Whatever you fail to change, you are destined to repeat. This is a crucial truth.

Let's say you get a great credit offer in the mail and decide to consolidate all your credit card debt onto that one new card. After all, it has a good interest rate and a generous credit line. So you pile all your debt on that one card and feel good about it because you have zero balances on the rest of your cards. But instead of shredding or cutting up those old cards, you keep them in your wallet. Before you know it, you've charged on them again, and you find yourself in more debt than you were before. It can be a painful lesson, but what you fail to change you're destined to repeat.

If we are honest with ourselves, we have to admit that shame often gets in the way of problem solving. We try to hide things from each other. Wives try to hide things from their husbands; husbands try to hide things from their wives; parents try to hide things from their kids; kids try to hide things from their parents; people try to hide things from the law and from the preacher. The number one reason we do this? Shame.

We worry about what people would think of us if they knew the truth. Shame is a crippling, paralyzing emotion. Adam hid because of his shame and the problem he had was sin.

If we want to move on to a new level and solve our problems, we have to get liberated from shame. You may have made a mess of your finances or a relationship. The truth can be painful, but it's like surgery. Going in for an operation can be frightening and painful, but it will help you in the long run. Admit to your present situation and let go of the shame.

As you take steps to solve your problem, **the second thing you must do is admit your present condition without blame.** We live in a society where everyone wants to blame someone else. No one wants to take responsibility.

Today's culture is setting up our young people for a world of hurt. We want to play games where nobody keeps score and nobody loses because we don't want anyone to "feel bad." Children need to learn early on that there are indeed winners and losers and a big part of that is how they play the game. If they don't learn this now, they will be like those people you read about in the news who file a lawsuit because they didn't get the job they wanted. Instead of realizing they didn't work hard enough or didn't have the experience, they want someone to blame.

This is a sad state of affairs. Each one of us needs to take responsibility for our own lives. We need to realize, this is my situation and I have to deal with it. I have to admit it without shame and without blame, and accept responsibility. It can be painful, but if you ever hope to solve the problem, you must admit your present condition.

Something powerfully liberating happens when you step up and accept responsibility. As long as a problem is in your mind, it can hide. But as soon as you grab hold of it and write it down or speak it, you've begun to capture that problem. You can look at it realistically and see it for what it is. Once you know what giant you're dealing with, you can discover what ammo you need. God will help you in this process.

MAKING PROGRESS

Okay, I admit, up to this point the problem-solving process has not been much fun for you. Let's change gears now and discover how you can really start to make progress.

The next very important step is to pray. Prayer is absolutely essential. You can't truly pray about a situation until you admit it and accept responsibility. If you deny responsibility, you can't pray honestly and truthfully about it. The very nature of prayer is to be honest and humble.

Prayer is absolutely essential.

You can't truly pray about a situation until you

admit it and accept responsibility.

James 4:2 (NKJV) says, "You do not have because you do not ask."

I dare say most of you are dealing with some things right now where the only thing you need to do is ask. There have been times when I've caught myself dragging along or worrying about a situation, and the Holy Spirit will remind me that I haven't even asked Him for help. I do not have because I did not ask!

"God, I need You to do something, I need You to handle this and show me what to do." Pray in faith, pray honestly, and *God will help you.* I encourage you to go ahead and ask, ask in faith, and you *will* receive an answer.

James 5:13 (NKJV) says, "Is anyone among you suffering? Let him pray."

You must pray on your own, but you also need to have some friends who will pray with you. I'm not saying to get rid of your other friends, but in tough times you want friends with faith. In addition to God, you need people in your life you can call on when you're in need of prayer. Sometimes the Holy Spirit will put you on their minds and they will pray for you before you even ask. We all need friends we can turn to for prayer.

I once heard about a man who was standing in line to greet the pastor after church. As he shook the pastor's hand, he asked, "Pastor, would you pray for my hearing?"

The pastor reached out, put his hands over both the man's ears and prayed with boldness, "Father in the name of Jesus, I pray that you touch this man, help his hearing and open his ears in Jesus' name. Amen!"

Then the pastor looked at the man and asked, "So, how's your hearing?"

"I don't know," the man replied. "It's not until Thursday."

If someone asks you to pray for them, be careful what you're asked to pray about!

But seriously, we need to pray in every way that we can pray. In 1 Corinthians 14:15 (NKJV), Paul writes, "I will pray with the spirit and I will also pray with the understanding." In the Amplified Bible, this same verse reads, "I will pray with my spirit, [by the Holy Spirit that is within me], but I will also pray [intelligently] with my mind and understanding."

Jude 1:20 (NKJV) says, "But you, beloved, building yourselves up on your most holy faith, praying in the Holy Spirit...."

You should pray with understanding, pray with the Spirit, and pray in faith as you cry out to God for help. Pray in every way possible and with firm confidence and faith, believing God will move and act on the situation. As you pray, ask for direction.

Proverbs 3:6 (NKJV) says, "In all your ways acknowledge Him, and He shall direct your paths."

You need direction and as you seek God, acknowledging Him in all you do, you can ask Him to direct your paths. God will give you insight.

I believe you should trust and rest in the Lord, but I also think it's important that you brainstorm. Brainstorming is literally flooding your brain with a storm of ideas as you search for a possible solution. God never said to stop using your brain. As you begin to read the Word, start to do research, do a Google search, ask friends and look for answers, I believe God will "light up" certain ideas.

This has happened to me as I've brainstormed about a problem. I was praying and thinking about possible solutions and suddenly — it was as if God lit up one of those ideas. The other ideas seemed to fade and I knew what to do. God gave me insight.

Don't be surprised if you get weary while brainstorming.

Matthew 7:7 (NLT) says, "Keep on asking, and you will receive what you ask for. Keep on seeking, and you will find. Keep on knocking, and the door will be opened to you."

When you're in that process of seeking, asking, knocking, and looking for answers, always keep your Bible nearby. It is God's Word. The Bible is literally God speaking to you.

While we're talking about solving problems, you should know that for every problem, there is a promise, whether it's specific or by principle. No matter what problem you have, God has already spoken about that situation.

Of course, there are times when you're looking for answers and you don't like what God says to do. You may not want to forgive someone who cheated or wronged you, but that's what the Bible tells you to do. If you want to have every advantage, you need to take God's Word to heart and apply His solutions to your problems.

The answer to your problem won't always come right away, but you must have faith that it *will* come. Once you ask in faith for God to give you wisdom and show you what to do, believe that He will.

I like to say, "I don't know, but I will know." Why? Because I believe that if I ask in faith and according to His Word, He will show me what to do. God is just looking for people who want to seek Him and ask for guidance.

Let's look at James 1:2-8 (NLT): "Dear brothers and sisters, when troubles come your way, consider it an opportunity for great joy. For you know that when your faith is tested, your endurance has a chance to grow. So let it grow, for when your endurance is fully developed you will be perfect and complete, needing nothing. If you need wisdom, ask our generous God, and He will give it to you. He will not rebuke you for asking. But when you ask Him, be sure that your faith is in God alone. Do not waver, for a person with divided loyalty is as unsettled as a wave of the sea that is blown and tossed by the wind. Such people should not expect to receive anything from the Lord. Their loyalty is divided between God and the world, and they are unstable in everything they do."

We have to endure what we don't enjoy. You've never had to "endure" an ice cream cone. We may not enjoy the process of having our faith tested, but if we approach it correctly, our endurance grows and we come out stronger on the other side.

In the process of problem solving, **the next step is often just to step away and "normalize" your life.** Finding the solution can be a tedious process and there are times when you just have to take a break. You aren't running away, or giving up, but as you step back you give your emotions a chance to clear out and calm down. God will refresh you.

There are still things to deal with, but give yourself a chance to "normalize," to take a break and just focus on everyday things: eat, sleep, work, play with your children. You aren't stopping your search for the solution, but you're giving your mind a chance to rest. It's amazing how you can be doing something totally unrelated and all of a sudden… there it is. You know what you should do. Then you can run back to God and He'll confirm it in His Word. He'll confirm it with peace in your spirit, and you will have assurance that you are on the right path.

Finally, you create an action plan. This is simply laying out the steps you should take and the specific actions necessary for solving the problem. Creating an action plan doesn't mean you are taking things into your own hands.

Continue to trust God that He will work it out. He will show you what to do. There may even be things about yourself He'll show you that need to be changed. If that's the case, you can be sure He will help you as you rely on Him.

Remember: God is your strength, He is your wisdom, and He gives you favor. There's nothing He cannot do, nothing that He cannot help, nothing that He cannot fix. Think about this for a moment. Tough times won't last if you and God are working together. God does His part and you do your part. There is no situation that is permanently locked. God can either unlock it, or show you the key. Either way, God is helping you. That is why I can say with total confidence… "tough times don't last!"

CHAPTER 6

DEALING WITH PROBLEMS AND FEAR

We've seen that the strength we need for our journey here on earth is *inner* strength. God, by His abundant grace, gives us this vital strength on the inside. We absolutely need that strength because without it, the pressures we face on the outside will cause us to collapse.

Although inner strength is crucial, we also need a broader sense of strength. This broader strength includes all the resources you have available, in both the natural and the spiritual: assets, abilities, supplies, advantages, armor, ammunition, and allies.

There will be times when you need one or more (maybe all!) of these resources, in addition to that God-given inner strength. Without them, you'll find yourself in trouble in the day of adversity.

In John 16:33 (NKJV), Jesus assured us those days will come. *"In the world you will have tribulation (trials, distress, and frustration), but be of good cheer, I have overcome the world."*

We have His promise that He'll give us the strength, the wisdom and the help that comes only from God to help us overcome the problems and adversities that are sure to come in this life.

One of my favorite verses in the Bible is Psalm 27:1 (NKJV): "The Lord is my light and my salvation, **whom shall I fear?** "The Lord is the strength of my life; of whom shall I be afraid?"

This is a verse to grab hold of and remember. When I need strength, I know the Lord is my strength. He's my light, my source and my salvation, which means I don't need to be fearful.

Psalm 46:1-2 (NKJV) says, "God is our refuge and strength, a very present help in trouble. Therefore **we will not fear**."

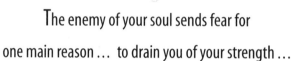

The enemy of your soul sends fear for
one main reason … to drain you of your strength …
Fear will cause the strength to seep right out of you if you let it.

Just reading this short verse, we realize two main things. First of all, we know there is going to be trouble. More importantly, we know that God will be right there with us. Not only will He be there, but He's promised to be our refuge and strength. Once we get that revelation and really believe it, we'll understand we don't ever have to be afraid.

Those same verses in the New Century Version read, "God is our protection and our strength. He always helps in times of trouble." Isn't that awesome? With God as my strength and shelter, I don't have to be afraid.

We already know tough times don't last, but this is even better news: God is our help, so we don't have to be afraid!

PROBLEMS AND FEAR

Let's consider problems for a moment. The trouble with problems is that they usually don't come by themselves. Problems tend to come in multiples or what I call a "package deal." No matter what type of problems show up, there's something else that is always part of the package... FEAR.

Maybe your problem is financial or related to your job. Maybe it's about your health or a relationship or your family. Whatever type of problem you may be dealing with, fear usually comes along for the ride.

If you go to the doctor for tests and he tells you he found a quiver in your liver, guess what? You not only have a quiver in your liver, you also have fear.

Fear tries to work its way into any situation where you are weak or susceptible. The enemy of your soul sends fear for one main reason… to drain you of your strength. You already know that strength is the issue, so this should make you sit up and take note. Fear will cause the strength to seep right out of you if you let it.

We're told in 2 Timothy 1:7 that God does not give us a spirit of fear, but of power, love, and a sound mind.

God is not the author of fear. Any time you sense fear in your life, you can be certain it IS NOT from God.

If you allow it, fear will steal your sleep at night. Fear will also keep you from thinking and speaking positive things. It will gnaw at you and try to steal your joy.

There's an evil design and purpose behind the fears that come into your life, whatever the circumstances. The enemy sends the spirit of fear to "team up" with problems and negative circumstances. He does this for one main purpose: to drain you of your strength. Why? Because without strength, you will faint in the day of adversity.

Think about this for a moment. If you open your mail and there's a bill that you owe but don't have the money to pay, that simple piece of paper can send your thoughts and emotions into turmoil. The bill that arrived in your mailbox is nothing but paper and ink. How can paper and ink keep you awake at night? What drives away the sleep is not a piece of paper, but the fear attached to it. That fear keeps you wondering, *How am I going to come up with the money? What if I can't pay it on time?*

It's crucially important for you to realize that strength is the issue and that fear threatens to rob you of strength. It's even more important for you to learn not to fear.

Unfortunately, human nature finds it very easy to fall into fear. A problem comes your way, and next thing you know, you're feeling fear.

It's almost automatic.

David, the Psalmist and great Old Testament king, knew all about fear. He faced some incredible obstacles in life, many of his own making, and he often had real reason to be afraid. There were numerous times he actually feared for his life. Yet David was continually building himself up and reminding himself NOT to be afraid. Throughout the Psalms we read David's words, "God is my light, my salvation, my strength, my shelter, my protection, my refuge, my help and my strength. I will not fear!"

We need to take a lesson from David and declare those same words, "I will not fear!" Even if you don't believe it at first, say it like you mean it and hang onto that thought.

Throughout Scripture we find some form of "fear not" 365 different times. That is one "fear not" for every day of the year.

In John 14:27b (AMP), Jesus says: "[*Stop allowing yourselves to be agitated and disturbed; and do not permit yourselves to be fearful and intimidated and cowardly and unsettled.]*"

This means the decision is ours. We can choose to fear… or NOT to fear. We can stop allowing fear to leave us agitated, disturbed, intimidated, cowardly and unsettled. It's a CHOICE.

You may be thinking this is easier said than done. What you must realize is that in order to fend off fear, a number of things need to be active and in place. *You need to have a reason not to fear.* It's not just about psyching yourself up and repeating, "I will not fear" a hundred times.

If you watch boxing, you'll see the boxers do a lot of "trash talking" in the promotional spots leading up to the match. There's a great deal of boasting about not being afraid of getting beat. Then it comes down to the match and those two guys are standing there staring each other down. One fighter has the eye of the tiger and it's drilling right through the other guy. This other boxer may be saying, "I ain't afraid," but inside… where it counts… he's feeling the fear. Guess who's going to win?

Know this: you can't just talk big. That might work for a little while, but it won't last. You can't simply talk yourself out of fear. There must be something in place and active in your life to give you reason to confidently say, "I will not be afraid."

STANDING FIRM

So what do you need in order to stay the course without fear knocking you down?

The first thing you need is what I call the "faith factor." This is exactly what I'm referring to when we talk about having a real revelation that God is your strength, light, salvation, shelter, refuge, protection and that *He will help you.* You must have faith and believe this!

You know that God is your light and your strength, but you still need to have a strategy.

How do you know this? It's in the Word of God. Faith comes by hearing and hearing by the Word of God (Romans 10:17 NKJV). You need to hear it, hear it, hear it… and the best way to hear it is right out of your own mouth. Declare it out loud: "God is my strength, He's my light, He's my salvation, He's my everything."

Declare it and believe it! Just saying the words won't change a thing if you don't grasp hold of this truth and believe it. If you're going to tackle life without fear, this needs to be settled once and for all on the inside. You must have the "faith factor" and truly believe that God is whatever you need.

The second thing you need is a strategy. You should have a God-given plan to deal with whatever comes your way, and that includes problems. We've already seen that God has His part and you have your part. You know that God is your light and your strength, but you still need to have a strategy.

In Chapter 5 we learned about "the essence of problem solving." We have to follow God's plan and incorporate our faith into that plan. This also means we have an active role to play. God will do His part when we do our part. We must always ask God to act and then ask Him to show us what to do. When you ask God for direction, He will provide that direction. He'll lead you and guide you as you step out and trust Him.

Your plan — your strategy — comes from God. When you ask God for help, that strategy comes through your spirit and through your mind because God is within you in the form of the Holy Spirit. He supplies power in your spirit to generate solutions whether you need help in your health, your family, your business or wherever.

Sometimes He'll only show you the next step instead of the whole process. I think the reason He shows me just the next step is because I might start to prioritize steps and say, "Well, that one's really not that important, let's get to the action." God orders our steps, He lights our path, and He will start to show you what you need to do. There's a power by the Holy Spirit within your spirit to generate solutions.

You can't get away with having irresponsible faith. The truth is that most of the time God expects you to do something. He sent us the Holy Spirit, but the Holy Spirit is our Helper. He's not the doer… that's our part.

I can assure you that there will be times, as you step out, that you'll think you just don't have the strength to do what needs to be done. That's when you fall back on the Word and build up your faith. Remind yourself, "I can do all things through Christ who strengthens me" (Philippians 4:13 NKJV)… "the Lord is the strength of my life" (Psalm 27:1 NKJV)… "God is our refuge and strength, a very present help in trouble" (Psalm 46:1-2 NKJV).

There are occasions when the Lord will act supernaturally on your behalf, as we read in 2 Chronicles 20:15. Those are the times when the Lord announces, "This battle is not yours. This battle's Mine. You just position yourself. You just sit over here, stand and see the salvation of the Lord. You don't need to fight; I'll take care of this one for you."

I've had those experiences and I love it when the Lord steps in this way. But most of the time it's a process. You need to ask God to act, and then you need to ask Him to show you what to do. Either way, God is helping you, setting you free, and giving you the victory.

Remember… there's nothing that is locked that God cannot unlock or show you the key. We have to be dependent upon God. We also need to have our "faith factor" and a strategy where we trust God to do His part and we do our part.

THE EMOTION OF FEAR

Fear is actually an emotional response to danger. That danger can be real or it may be perceived, but either way your emotional response is real.

Let's take the case of real danger. Say you're out in the yard trimming hedges and suddenly you hear loud buzzing. Without realizing it, you disturbed a wasp nest and look out, here they come! You can't just stand there saying, "Jesus, protect me." You'd better have a plan and I would suggest you run, jump in the pool, or something, but GET OUT OF THERE! That's real danger and it would create sudden fear.

Then we have perceived danger, which also causes fear. Hollywood has made a fortune by creating perceived fear. You watch a thriller movie and there's always a bad guy chasing some poor victim. He chases her all the way up the stairs, and there's a big knock-down-drag-out on the top floor. Someone jumps out and hits the bad guy in the head with an ax; he reels over to the window and tumbles out. He hits the sidewalk and everyone in the audience (including you!) is relieved. Whew! He's gone! But you know what always happens in those movies… just when everyone thinks they're safe and nobody's looking, the bad guy staggers to his feet, pulls the ax out of his head and the chase is on again. You're just watching, but your heart is pounding and you're screaming at the screen like it was actually happening. You've just scared yourself silly over something that isn't even real. This is just one example, but I think we need to be careful not to feed fear in our lives.

Mark Twain put it this way: "I've had thousands of crises in my life, and two of them were actually real."

Fear is an emotional response to danger, be it real or perceived. Anxiety and panic may be out-of-proportion responses to an actual danger or threat. Just consider how some people respond to spiders. Studies have been done for years, and all the results are in: screaming does not kill spiders. Guess what? Follow-up studies reveal that screaming doesn't even scare them!

Sometimes we panic over something and use our emotions as our first line of defense. A problem crops up and the first thing we do is send our emotions out as the first wave to attack the problem.

You can't trust your emotions that way. Emotions have to be kept in the right place. You can't allow them to be your first response to troubles that come into your life. Emotion has its place, but it is ineffective in dealing with problems.

Jesus addressed this directly when He asked the disciples, *"Which of you by worrying can change anything?"*

If you're staying awake at night worrying because the doctor said you've got a quiver in your liver, you might as well go to sleep. Psalm 121:3 says, "He who watches over you neither slumbers nor sleeps...." I've heard it put this way: if He's staying awake, there's no reason for the both of us to stay up! Instead of letting fear drag you around, you can rest in Him.

HELP IS ON THE WAY

Many times God brings us help in the form of a person. God uses people to bring a word of encouragement, to offer wisdom, and to provide an actual helping hand. Of course, this doesn't mean you should listen to just anyone who comes along. Some people like to share what they think God intends for you, but their words will bear witness in your spirit if the message is really from God. It will line up with God's Word and you will feel peace from the Holy Spirit.

In 2 Corinthians 7:5 (NLT), Paul talks about the trials they faced. "When we arrived in Macedonia, there was no rest for us. Outside there was conflict from every direction, and inside there was fear." That same verse in the NKJV reads: "Outside were conflicts, inside were fears."

That's right... their problems were combined with fear.

But God made sure help was on the way, as we read in 2 Corinthians 7:6 (NLT). "But God, who encourages those who are discouraged, encouraged us by the arrival of Titus."

God sent Titus, another believer, to help and encourage Paul and his group.

Even though you may feel like there are troubles on every side and fear welling up inside, rest assured that God will send help. He'll send someone at just the right time; sometimes He will even use your pastor!

Notice what the Scripture says about Titus: "His presence was a joy, but so was the news he brought...." This was someone who brought joy and comfort just by being present and by the words he spoke.

We all like getting answers to our prayers, but how amazing is it to think you could BE an answer to prayer?

I'm sure you know that not everyone brings joy when they show up. That's exactly why we can be thankful for Caller ID. But seriously, we each need to be aware of the message we're sending through our presence and our words so that we bring peace and encouragement into the lives of others.

There are times when God uses us as an answer to someone else's prayer for help. We all like getting answers to our prayers, but how amazing is it to think you could BE an answer to prayer?

You will see that the more you allow God to work in your life, the more He will use you to help and impact other people. This happens when you grow beyond the place where it's all about "me and mine." You don't have to have a degree or be "super spiritual" for this to happen. You just have to subject yourself to God.

If God is going to use you in someone's life, you can't just barge in. You don't go to the mall or walk up to someone in a restaurant and say, "Excuse me. You look like you're troubled," or "Boy, have I got news for you!"

God doesn't work that way and we shouldn't either. If you pay attention to His moving, you'll find the Holy Spirit will set up situations for you to minister to other people. When you respond to His moving, you can be sure the timing is always right. I dare you to pray every day, "*God, use me in some way to help someone today. May my presence and my words bring joy to somebody.*"

It may sound simple, but this is all you have to do. You don't have to lurk around looking for someone to bless. Just go through your day and the Lord will show you. You'll run into people and situations and you will know what to do and say. Your presence and your words will bring joy to them.

Here's a formula from Scripture that will guide you in talking to people. Isaiah 35:4 (NKJV) says, "Say to those who are fearful-hearted, 'Be strong, do not fear! Behold your God will come with vengeance; with the recompense of God; He will come and save you.'"

You can't go wrong if you tell someone, "Be strong. Don't be afraid. God will come and save you."

Obviously, you don't know how God is going to do this, but that doesn't need to stop you from speaking hope to someone. You don't have to know how God will work; that isn't your burden. But based on His Word and His track record, you can say, "Be strong and don't be afraid. He will come and save you!"

People may ask, "How is He going to do that?" You can tell them, "I don't know. But what I do know is that He's done it before, and He's done it for me, and I know He will do it for you."

You have to get to that place in your daily life where you believe God and take Him at His Word. Believe He'll come through. Believe He'll unlock what needs to be unlocked or show you the key to do it yourself. Believe He will change things!

Of course, you really can't help other people if you don't believe this in your own life. You can't give what you don't have. No, you don't have to be "perfect" before you can help someone else, but you need to have certain basic truths settled beyond any doubt. You have to be assured that God is your strength, that He will help you, and that you don't have to fear.

You need to know this in spite of all the "what ifs" that come along. "What if" the market crashes? "What if" gas prices keep going up? "What if" the terrorists strike again? "What if" this, "what if" that? You know you don't have to be afraid, because God is your strength, your source, your light, your provider, your healer, your counselor, and your protector.

Things happen. We all get stunned by life at one time or another. But the thing is, maturity is measured by recovery time. We're either up or we're getting up!

2 Corinthians 1:3-4 (NLT) says: "All praise to God, the Father of our Lord Jesus Christ. God is our merciful Father and the source of all comfort. He comforts us in all our troubles so that we can comfort others."

In the Message Bible, those verses read, "All praise to the God and Father of our Master Jesus the Messiah! Father of all mercy! God of all healing counsel! He comes alongside us when we go through hard times, and before you know it, He brings us alongside someone else who is going through hard times so that we can be there for that person just as God was there for us."

These verses make it very clear that we are to comfort others with the same comfort God has shown us. We're literally passing on what God has given us.

Some of you have already been there. You've been through tough times and you remember what it was like to think, "Everything is falling apart. What if this doesn't work? How am I going to make it?" But now you're out of that difficult time and you can say without hesitation that God brought you through. Now it's your chance to help someone else. I think it's wrong for you to clam up and not be willing to help others when God gave you victory in some area of your life.

I challenge you to get this settled in your heart, to know for certain that God is the strength of your life and that you don't have to be afraid. Then I dare you to ask God to use you to help someone else by passing on the comfort you have received.

One thing you absolutely want to guard against is speaking discouragement to someone, or increasing their fear. Just like Titus, your presence and your words should bring strength because of God working through you. Tearing down and discouraging, increasing fear... those actions are the devil's work. When you speak, it should only be to build someone up. Either build up or hush up! We've made it a point to teach that to our children, but it also applies to our Christian walk. The world would be a happier place, not to mention a quieter place, if everyone either built up or hushed up.

Your presence and your words will either help or hinder somebody. Let's make sure that they are helpful and positive. ⤐

CHAPTER 7

PEACE IN THE MIDST OF CHALLENGES

If anyone knew about facing fear and difficulties, it was King David. His life reads like a made-for-television movie: love, lust, deception, family secrets, victory and loss, elation and deepest despair.

At one point, his own son, Absalom, turned traitor and gathered a group of rebels to try and steal the kingdom from him. Yet even as David suffered his son's betrayal and fled for his very life, somehow he had peace.

Things couldn't get much worse, but it was during these dark, distressing circumstances that David wrote in Psalm 4:7-8 (NKJV), "You have put gladness in my heart, more than in the season that their grain and wine increased. I will both lie down in peace and sleep; for You alone, O Lord, make me dwell in safety."

What God did for David, He can do for you. Even during hard times, God is able to put gladness in your heart, so that you can lie down in peace and sleep.

The Hebrew word for "peace" is the word "shalom." It has to do with wholeness and safety. The shalom peace that comes from God means a sense of having nothing missing and nothing broken. Like David, you can maintain a sense of peace even when things in life are far from perfect.

In John 16:33 (AMP), Jesus said, "*I have told you these things, so that in*

Me you may have [perfect] peace and confidence. In the world you have tribulation and trials and distress and frustration; but be of good cheer [take courage; be confident, certain, undaunted]! For I have overcome the world. [I have deprived it of power to harm you and have conquered it for you.]"

Real peace springs from having hope even in the midst of troubles and conflicts. The only way to have that kind of peace is through God.

There are many cheap imitations for peace in this world. Desperate people search for peace in many different places, but it can't be found in a bottle, in a pill, in a relationship, a cause, or an activity. True peace isn't naturally found on this planet. It has to be imported. It's a supplement from heaven. It's not natural; it's supernatural, and God is the source.

Keep in mind that peace is not the absence of problems. Real peace springs from having hope even in the midst of troubles and conflicts. The only way to have that kind of peace is through God.

Paul wrote in Philippians 4:7 (AMP), "And God's peace [shall be yours, that tranquil state of a soul assured of its salvation through Christ, and so fearing nothing from God and being content with its earthly lot of whatever sort that is, that peace] which transcends all understanding shall garrison and mount guard over your hearts and minds in Christ Jesus."

The reality is, you are going to have difficulties in this life. We all do. It just goes with the turf, so it is important that you also have peace that will guard your heart and your mind.

REAL PEACE, NOT AN IMITATION

The New Testament word for peace means "rest, quiet, contentment, to feel full and have fulfillment."

Romans 5:1 (NKJV) says, "Therefore, having been justified by faith, we have peace with God through our Lord Jesus Christ."

Ephesians 2:14 (NKJV) says, "For He Himself is our peace."

In Isaiah 9:6 and in several other passages of Scripture, Jesus is referred to as "the Prince of Peace."

It's obvious from these verses that Jesus is the connection we need to find peace.

2 Corinthians 5:18-21 (NKJV) says, "Now all things are of God, Who has reconciled us to Himself through Jesus Christ...."

This same verse in the New Century Version reads, "Through Christ, God made peace between us and Himself."

By sending Christ to die for our sins, God paved the way for us to be at peace with Him. He sent Jesus as our substitute to pay the debt of sin in our place. When we, through faith, believe and accept what Christ did for us, God's peace begins to flow in our lives. The world has substitutes for peace, but we can have peace because we have a substitute.

You probably know Christians who aren't at peace. You may have found yourself lacking peace at times. This is because God's peace only comes through relationship and trust in Him. It's always available, but it's not automatic.

In Isaiah 48:22 (NKJV), as well as three other places in the book of Isaiah, we read, "'There is no peace,' says the Lord, 'for the wicked.'"

Many believers read that verse and think it doesn't apply to them because it refers to "the wicked." But in this scenario, "wicked" isn't just about non-believers. To be wicked means to be wrong or ungodly. It's certainly possible to be a Christian and still think or act in a wrong or ungodly way, which quickly drains your peace.

If we want peace *from* God, we have to be at peace *with* God. Any time you feel a lack of peace in your life, check your actions, thoughts, and words. Take an honest look at your relationship with God. There's a bumper sticker that puts this in perspective very simply: **No God, no peace. Know God, know peace.**

Unless you have peace with God, it's impossible to be at peace with yourself or at peace with others. Your internal affects your external. If something is missing in your relationship with God, you'll feel the absence of peace. Peace — or the lack of it — is one sure way to gauge the health of your spiritual relationship.

You have to guard and nurture your relationship with God because the more you do this, the more peace you will have.

Romans 14:17 (NKJV) says. "…for the kingdom of God is not eating and drinking, but righteousness and peace and joy in the Holy Spirit."

If you are in relationship with God, you are in the kingdom, and if peace is in the kingdom, you will have peace in your life!

STAY HUMBLE

In Psalm 37:11 (NKJV) we read, "But the meek shall inherit the earth and shall delight themselves in the abundance of peace."

If the meek — the humble — are going to enjoy an abundance of peace, I'll choose to be meek. Sign me up! Which bus do we get on to Meekville?

Unfortunately, meekness and humility are greatly misunderstood, particularly in today's culture. We tend to think of meekness, or humility, as weakness, yet that's not how God views it.

Moses was meek. Numbers 12:3 (NKJV) says, "Now the man Moses was very humble, more than all men who were on the face of the earth."

Paul was meek. In 2 Corinthians 10:1 (NKJV), he writes, "Now I, Paul, myself am pleading with you by the meekness and gentleness of Christ — Who in presence am lowly among you, but being absent am bold toward you."

Jesus was meek. In Matthew 11:29 (NKJV) He said, *"Take My yoke upon you and learn from Me, for I am gentle (meek) and lowly in heart, and you will find rest for your souls."*

Moses, Paul, and Jesus certainly weren't weak, yet the Bible says they were meek.

Colossians 3:12 (NKJV) tells us, "Therefore, as the elect of God, holy and beloved, put on tender mercies, kindness, humility, meekness, long suffering…"

Meekness is actually something you can cultivate. It is strength and courage under control, coupled with kindness. Perhaps the best definition of meekness is this: Having an attitude of humility toward God, gentleness toward men, and recognition that God is in control. Understanding that God is in control should give you both hope and peace.

Perhaps the best definition of meekness is this:

Having an attitude of humility toward God, gentleness toward men,

and recognition that God is in control.

Let's look at an extreme example of humility in action. In 2 Chronicles 20, we find King Jehoshaphat, king of Judah and Jerusalem. At that time Israel was divided into the northern and southern territories, with the southern territory called Judah. The city of Jerusalem lay within Judah.

King Jehoshaphat learns the frightening news that the armies of three enemy nations were marching towards him to do battle. He was afraid, yet immediately he sought the Lord for guidance.

2 Chronicles 20:9 (NLT) says, "They said, 'Whenever we are faced with any calamity such as war, plague, or famine, we can come to stand in your presence before this temple where your name is honored. We can cry out to you to save us, and you will hear us and rescue us.'"

Verse 12 continues, "O our God, won't you stop them? We are powerless against this mighty army that is about to attack us. We do not know what to do, but we are looking to you for help."

In verse 15, the Lord spoke through a young man, "He said, 'Listen, all you people of Judah and Jerusalem! Listen, King Jehoshaphat! This is what the Lord says: Do not be afraid! Don't be discouraged by this mighty army, for the battle is not yours, but God's.'"

With his confidence firmly in God, King Jehoshaphat made a very humble move. He appointed singers — that's right, singers, not soldiers — to go in front of his army, to sing and praise God as they went.

Miraculously, the approaching armies became confused and instead of attacking King Jehoshaphat's people, they turned on each other and fought until all were dead. God's people simply sang, stood still, and watched their enemies destroy one another.

Verse 25 reads, "King Jehoshaphat and his men went out to gather the plunder. They found vast amounts of equipment, clothing, and other valuables — more than they could carry. There was so much plunder that it took them three days just to collect it all! On the fourth day they gathered in the Valley of Blessing, which got its name that day because the people praised and thanked the Lord there. It is still called the Valley of Blessing today. Then all the men returned to Jerusalem, with Jehoshaphat leading them, overjoyed that the Lord had given them victory over their enemies. They marched into Jerusalem to the music of harps, lyres, and trumpets, and they proceeded to the temple of the Lord. When all the surrounding kingdoms heard that the Lord himself had fought against the enemies of Israel, the fear of God came over them. So Jehoshaphat's kingdom was at peace, for his God had given him rest on every side."

Not only did God provide peace and rest "on every side," but He also provided plunder and provision for His people. All this because they recognized that He was in control, trusted Him and acted in humility.

When you humble yourself before a sovereign God, He will come through for you. Recognize that God is in control and make it a point to live each day in an attitude of humility with God as your source.

HOW TO HOLD ONTO PEACE

In Luke 19, we read of Jesus approaching Jerusalem before Palm Sunday. Because of His vantage point, He had a good view of the city, and as He looked out over it, He wept audibly.

In Luke 19:42 (NKJV), He said, *"If you had known, even you, especially in this your day, the things that make for your peace! But now they are hidden from your eyes."*

Jesus wept for the people because sin clouded their eyes and they didn't realize what would bring them real peace. This also applies to us because without peace, we will have spiritual blindness, captivity and destruction. This can be true even for Christians.

Psalm 34:14 (NKJV) says, "Depart from evil and do good; seek peace and pursue it."

We already know peace comes through relationship with God, so if we are to seek peace, we must actively pursue God. If you are not in relationship with God, He will not give you peace. He may give you mercy and protect you, simply because He is good. But if you want peace — the kind of peace that will comfort you no matter what happens in life — you need Jesus, the Prince of Peace, in your heart.

Psalm 29:11 says, "The Lord will give strength to His people. The Lord will bless His people with peace."

If you belong to Him, God wants to give you both strength and peace. Talk about a package deal!

In 1 Corinthians 1:3 (NKJV) Paul writes, "Grace to you and peace from God our Father and the Lord Jesus Christ."

Romans 15:13 (NKJV) reads, "Now may the God of hope fill you with all joy and peace in believing, that you may abound in hope by the power of the Holy Spirit."

Grace and peace… joy and peace… these are the kinds of package deals we need every day, but especially during tough times. God's peace can literally hold us in "protective custody" as we stay close to Him.

In John 14:1 (NLT) Jesus says, *"Don't be troubled. You trust God, now trust in Me."*

If we want to have peace and not be troubled, we must practice trusting — which is simply another word for believing — in God and what He says in His Word.

No matter how you arrived at your present reality, take the situation to

God in prayer. Too many times, we want to talk about and analyze what's happening, but instead, we should shape our worries and concerns into prayers. If you want to worry less, pray more!

We must stop viewing our current challenges as permanent fixtures in life. This can be easier said than done when dealing with serious medical, financial or relationship issues. But if we think of what's happening now as permanent, we surrender our hope, and hope is essential because PEACE SPRINGS FROM HOPE.

Hope gives your faith something to work with, so never lose hope!

CHAPTER 8

OVERCOMING STORMS IN LIFE

As you walk out your faith day by day, you can be sure that challenges will come, but you've learned that you don't have to be afraid because the Lord is the strength of your life.

Tough times affect each of us, but that's never the end of the story. Why? *Because we have a strength greater than our own and we have a God we can always rely on.*

This much I know: God forever was God and forever will be God. He's the same yesterday, today, and forever. He's got everything in control. Nothing takes Him by surprise. There is no lack in God, no weakness in God, no lapse in God. He is my light and my salvation; He is the strength of my life, and I will not be afraid. I know that God is faithful and I also know that tough times don't last!

1 Corinthians 10:13 (Message) says, "No test or temptation that comes your way is beyond the course of what others have had to face. All you need to remember is that God will never let you down; He'll never let you be pushed past your limit; He'll always be there to help you come through it."

HANDLING THE STORMS OF LIFE

God never tried to hide the fact that storms are part of life. The Bible talks about storms in several different places in a figurative way. Although some of these verses describe physical storms, complete with wind, waves and rain, they are also talking about tough times, troubles, and challenges that come into our lives.

Storms come, but here's the good news… they don't last forever!

As I stated earlier, 2004 was a year of multiple hurricanes all across the state of Florida. They came, but thank God, they went. We can learn important lessons from taking a look at real storms and how they apply, in a figurative way, to tough times in life.

Through faith and believing in the power of God, you take a stand and speak out against that storm, that challenge, whatever it may be.

If you want to live in victory, there are several key things you need to do when a storm strikes your life. **The first thing you should do is rebuke that storm.** Rebuke it. You probably don't use the word "rebuke" very often, but what I'm referring to here is a command of faith. Through faith and believing in the power of God, you take a stand and speak out against that storm, that challenge, whatever it may be. You literally say, "Stop it! Just stop now, in the name of Jesus!"

You may not fully understand this principle yet, but as a believer you have authority in the name of Jesus. There is tremendous power in His name. Jesus said you can even speak to mountains and command them to move. You may not need to move an actual mountain, but there are times you're facing obstacles and situations that feel just as enormous and solid as a mountain of rock. You can rebuke them in Jesus' name by speaking the command of faith.

In Mark 4, we read the account of a major storm that arose when Jesus and His disciples were in a boat crossing a large lake. One translation, the

Amplified, describes it as a "furious storm of wind of hurricane proportions." Rain and wind were lashing the boat, and waves were spilling over the sides, threatening to sink it.

Despite the storm, Jesus was asleep in the stern of the boat. The Bible doesn't tell us how long the disciples let Him sleep, but it does say that by the time they woke Him up, they were asking, "Don't you care that we are perishing?" No doubt they were scared for their lives.

Jesus got up and according to Scripture, the first thing He did was rebuke the wind. He spoke the command of faith and essentially said, "Stop it!" And the wind stopped. Then He spoke to the waves saying, "Peace, be still!" (Mark 4:39) The waves were simply responding to the wind, but at His words, they settled into a great calm.

Jesus then spoke to the disciples and asked them why they were so fearful, why they had no faith. (I think He probably said something like, "Just cool your jets." At least, that would be my paraphrase if I were writing it.)

The Bible tells us that after Jesus calmed the storm, the disciples were filled with "great awe." They witnessed firsthand the incredible power in Jesus' spoken words. This amazing lesson is certainly worth remembering in our own storms of life. When the winds and waves of adversity and trial are swirling around you, speak up and rebuke that situation in the name of Jesus.

The second thing that you should do when faced with a storm is to repent. It's human nature when problems arise to blame them on somebody or something other than yourself. Of course, there are times when you find yourself in a situation that was absolutely no fault of your own. But many situations are a direct result of something you said, did, or were involved in that isn't pleasing to God. If you have done something wrong, you need to acknowledge it, turn from it, and repent.

In the Old Testament, we read about the prophet Jonah, who had the call of God on his life. The Lord instructed Jonah to go to the city of Nineveh and preach righteousness. Jonah, however, had other plans.

In direct disobedience to God's word, he went and found a ship that was sailing to a remote trading place, paid his fare and went aboard. He was blatantly fleeing from God and God's command.

Jonah 1:4 (AMP) says, "But the Lord sent out a great wind upon the sea, and there was a violent tempest on the sea so that the ship was about to be broken."

In the following verses, we read that the sailors were afraid and began praying to all their gods. Frantically, they hurled the cargo overboard into the sea, hoping to lighten the load and keep the boat from sinking. Meanwhile, Jonah was fast asleep below deck.

After the captain discovered him, the men quickly figured out that if he wasn't praying or trying to help, he must be the problem. Confronted with the truth, Jonah confessed that he was running from God. Jonah said to them, "Take me up and cast me into the sea; so shall the sea become calm for you, for I know that it is because of me that this great tempest has come upon you."

To their credit, the sailors still tried hard to row and bring the ship to land, but when the storm became even more violent, they finally took Jonah's suggestion and threw him into the sea. Once they did, the storm ceased.

God hadn't given up on Jonah, and sent a big fish to swallow him. Jonah 1:17 tells us Jonah was in the belly of the fish for three days and three nights. That's a lot of time to think.

Jonah finally came to the place where he repented and said, "Okay, God, I'll do what you told me to do." Scripture says the Lord "spoke to the fish and it vomited out Jonah upon the dry land." Hopefully, it won't take such dramatic circumstances for us to realize when we need to repent.

The third thing you may need to do in a storm is to ride it out. We read a perfect example of this in Acts 27.

Paul was under house arrest and being shipped, along with other prisoners, to Rome. Because of the time of year, navigation was dangerous. Paul actually tried to warn the centurion responsible for guarding him that this journey was a bad idea. The owner of the ship was determined to sail, however, so they left port and soon enough were caught up in a powerful storm.

Scripture says that the crew threw the freight overboard and after many days of raging seas had abandoned all hope of being saved. After fourteen days of being battered by the storm, the sailors decided to try and strike out for land by taking the small "rescue" boat. Paul told them they would all survive if they just stayed together on the ship. As long as they stayed put and rode it out, he promised they would survive… and they did. Not one soul perished. Every person on board escaped safely to land, even after the boat ran aground and broke up.

Sometimes you just need to get yourself a roll of waterproof duct tape, strap yourself to the stern and just hang on. Just ride it out! No storm lasts forever.

WORTH REMEMBERING

In addition to these three major steps, there are several other things you may need to do when facing a storm. Let's consider them.

Respond. When you have a storm in your life you need to **respond, not react.** Reacting is emotional, and you've already learned that you don't send your emotions out as the first wave of attack in response to a problem. Instead of reacting based on your emotions, you want to take the time necessary to "get a grip" and seek God. If you do this first, He'll show you how to respond with the right tools and in the right way.

Review. Sometimes the best course of action is to step back and **review** the situation with God's help. Rather than just jumping ahead and doing something, review the problem first and ask God to open your eyes so you have a clear view of what is really happening. Be honest with yourself and be honest with God. Ask Him to show you and expect that He will.

Reinforce. In tough times, it's all too easy to focus on that, but you need to look beyond the problem for the strong, positive things in your life and then fortify them even more. Find the good things, the godly things, the right things, and **reinforce** those things in your life. During the storm described in Acts 27, the sailors used chains to try and reinforce the boat to help it hold up. Most of us have "fluff" in our lives that serves no useful purpose and even weakens us. (If you aren't sure what "fluff" is in your life, ask God to make it clear.) When times are challenging, you need to make a point to let go of the fluff. Get hold of — and strengthen — the good things (and people), and in turn, they can help you become stronger.

Reduce. Realize that you may have to cut back on some things in order to move in the right direction. You may need to **reduce** the energy, time, and money you're putting into different things. For example, if you want to reduce debt, you have to cut out extravagance and unnecessary expenses. If you want to get closer to God, you may need to reduce the amount of time you spend watching television. If you want to improve your family relationship, you may need to reduce the time you spend working late. Ask God to show you if there are areas where you need to cut back and reduce, and then act when He shows you.

Reorder. When you're in a storm, you realize what's really important. Relationships are always more important than anything material, and one relationship must have first place. You need to make sure your priorities are right, so **reorder** them if they're out of place. I can assure you, *nothing will be in order unless you have your first priority settled. God must be first in your life.*

Reconcile. You don't need strife in your life at any time, but during tough times, you especially don't need to hold onto any type of strife or bitterness. Get it out of your life, out of your home, out of your marriage, out of your relationships, and out of your finances. Forgive and let it go! **Reconcile** whatever you need to and be done with it. Accept that God has been so good to you, you can afford to just let some things go. Don't cling to anger and unforgiveness. Even when someone has truly wronged you, holding onto it only hurts you. Strife will just make your storm worse. So, let it go!

Research. You must remember that problems are not solved on the same level on which they were created. To find the answers, you must take it to another level, and that usually involves some **research**. When you're dealing with problems, realize that doing research and learning more about the situation can make a real difference.

Remain. When you've done all you know to do, sometimes you just have to stand still and **remain** in place. In Ephesians 6:13-14, Paul exhorts us with this principle, "…having done all, to stand… stand."

When a rabbit senses a threat, he will freeze in his tracks. While it may appear he's just sitting there, he's actually checking out options and considering routes of escape. Sometimes, you need to do the same. *Just be still, get a grip, and hold on.* Too often, we try to "do something" and it doesn't necessarily help the situation; it can even make things worse. Don't overlook the value of looking to God and waiting before you make a move.

Jesus made it quite plain. You can be wise or foolish.... If you're wise, you will make the decision to follow God and build your life on Him.

Reach. Sometimes you're so busy bailing or treading water in the storm that you forget you have a future and a hope. At those moments, you need to lift up your eyes, focus on God, and realize you aren't going to live forever under your present problems and pressures. I encourage you to take hope and **reach** toward that brighter future.

FIRM FOUNDATION

When it comes to your future, there are two foundations that you can build on.

Jesus explains this in detail in Matthew 7:24-27 (NLT): "*Anyone who listens to My teachings and obeys Me is wise, like a person who builds a house on solid rock. Though the rain comes in torrents and the flood waters rise and the winds beat against that house, it won't collapse because it is built on rock. But anyone who hears My teaching and ignores it is foolish, like a person who builds a house on sand. When the rains and floods come and the winds beat against that house, it will fall with a mighty crash.*"

You choose the foundation on which you build your life: rock or sand. Jesus made it quite plain. You can be wise or foolish. Scripture gives us clear direction, but you choose what to do with those instructions. If you're wise, you will make the decision to follow God and build your life on Him. The foolish person has the same opportunity, but decides to go his own way. Whether he knows it or not, he's choosing to build on sand.

In Matthew 7:21-23 (NLT), Jesus says: *"Not all people who sound religious are really godly. They may refer to me as 'Lord,' but they still won't enter the Kingdom of Heaven. The decisive issue is whether they obey my Father in heaven. On judgment day many will tell Me, 'Lord, Lord, we prophesied in your name and cast out demons in your name, and performed many miracles in your name,' but I will reply, 'I never knew you. Go away. The things you did were unauthorized.'"*

What He's really saying is that there's a difference — a crucial difference — between "playing church" and truly following after God's way. Some people believe all they need to do is go to church and have a "honk if you love Jesus" bumper sticker on their car.

In Matthew 7:13-14, Jesus is talking about two specific groups of people. He says that there are two paths and two gates, and describes them as a type of dividing line. He tells us that the larger group of people will choose the path that is the way of the world, the path of least resistance, which ultimately leads to destruction. The second smaller group of people decides to take the narrow path and enter through the gate that leads to life. They choose to go God's way.

Jesus may have been talking about this 2,000 years ago, but we still face those same choices today.

GET PREPARED

If you aren't prepared for a storm, it can be devastating. As a minister once said, "Trying to build a foundation during the flood is very difficult to do."

You need some on-going preparation so you're standing on solid ground and ready when storms hit. Sometimes we have warnings; other times the storm seems to strike out of the blue. Either way, if you're not prepared, the results can be catastrophic.

Thinking back on the hurricanes of 2004, I pray we never have another one ever, ever, ever! But I can remember it clearly. Our house is a block home and only about ten years old, so we felt we were in good shape, but we were still doing everything we knew to prepare. We boarded up windows and had a generator running and our kids actually enjoyed the hurricane. The room was dark and cozy and they were eating snacks and watching old Disney movies. Meanwhile, I was out on the front porch watching the winds and rain. I actually saw a tree fall on my neighbor's car. I started speaking to my trees and declaring, "You stand and you do not fall!"

Barry Mitchell is a missionary and a precious friend of our family. He pastors a church and a Bible School in Estonia, a former Soviet state, by the Baltic. I've had the privilege to go visit there and teach a couple of times, and he comes here every year or so to visit with us. Barry and his wife, Brenda, have been in Estonia about sixteen years now and are just as happy as can be. They know that they were called to that nation, and they're having a great impact on the people there.

During a recent visit, Barry was telling me that they had been renting a tiny place for years, but finally had enough money to build a house.

"I've got to tell you about my house," he said. "I go out to the construction site and they're building the walls with these HUGE blocks. They've got this wall going up with these huge blocks. Inside of that wall are six to eight inches of insulation, and then another huge block. The walls are incredibly thick."

He asked the contractor if that wasn't overkill and an added expense. The contractor just said, "You Americans!" and proceeded to laugh about American-built homes.

When it comes to the storms of life, "this little piggy" wants to go stay with "that little piggy" in the house in Estonia! Anybody can huff and puff and try to blow that house down, but it's built to last. The little piggies in that house are safe inside eating snacks and playing Uno. I bet they're not even afraid.

Whether we're talking hurricanes or the figurative storms of life, both of them bring fear and the potential for devastation. Here is what we have to remember: if we build on the Rock, we will not fall.

In Matthew 7:25 (NKJV), Jesus said, *"And the rain descended, the floods came, and the winds blew and beat on that house, and it DID NOT FALL, for it was founded on the rock."*

Luke 6:48 (NKJV) says, *"He is like a man building a house who dug deep and laid the foundation on the rock, and when the flood arose, the stream beat vehemently against that house, and could not shake it...."*

Not only did the house not fall, but the storm couldn't even shake it because it was on a foundation of rock.

Let's return to Matthew 7:24 (NKJV) and look at that verse again. Jesus says, *"Therefore whoever hears these sayings of Mine, and does them, I will liken him to a wise man who built his house on the rock."*

If you want your house — your life — to stand firm, you must be wise and build on the rock. Throughout life, tough times come and tough times go. They wage war against you and try to batter your life, but if you are fortified and strengthened, you won't fall. You'll know the storm is there because you can feel it, but you won't be shaken and you won't be destroyed.

This kind of strength doesn't come from just showing up at church or wearing a Christian T-shirt. It comes through building your life upon a solid foundation, and the only way to do this is to **hear** the sayings of Jesus from His Word and to **do** them! Be wise and dig deep. Make God's truths the core of your life, the very foundation upon which you build your life. Then you will have a life that will stand the test of storms!

Psalm 125:1 (NKJV) tells us, "Those who trust in the Lord are like Mount Zion, which cannot be moved, but abides forever."

In Matthew 7:27 (NKJV), when Jesus was talking about the man who built his house on sand, He says, *"And the rain descended, the floods came, and the winds blew and beat on that house, and it fell; and great was its fall."* Another translation (TEV) says, *"What a terrible fall it was."*

Not only did the house fall, but it was a disastrous fall.

The storm alone wasn't what caused the fall. The problem was that the house was built on nothing but sand, just like *"everyone who hears these things of Mine, and does not do them..."* (verse 26).

The Message Bible puts it plainly: *"But if you just use my words and Bible studies and don't work them into your life, you are like a stupid carpenter who built his house on the sandy beach. When a storm rolled in and the waves came up, it collapsed like a house of cards."*

The Word of God will **help** you and **equip** you. It can give you what you need to withstand the storms of life… if you hear it and obey. The foolish man builds his house on sand, which means he hears the Word (and he may even *believe* it), but he *does not do* what the Word says to do.

Make God's truths the core of your life,

the very foundation upon which you build your life.

Then you will have a life that will stand the test of storms!

The Word of God literally gives us what we need for every situation, but we need to obey and apply it. You can own the best fire extinguisher ever made, but if you don't use it when a fire breaks out, it's not going to help you at all.

Make no mistake: *you choose how you build your life, and you've been given the tools to build it so it will stand.* You cannot act like the teachings of Jesus don't matter. If you listen to the secular media, they would have you think that nobody's a Christian anymore. The truth is that the body of Christ is the largest affinity group and religion in the world, and is growing at a rapid pace all over this planet.

We're constantly hearing through the media that Christianity is "close-minded" and "out-dated" and that Jesus' teachings don't matter in today's modern world. That's a very old lie. Think back to the Garden of Eden when the devil, the great deceiver himself, enticed Eve by saying, "God didn't really mean that… it won't matter.…" He keeps using the same lie because it still works.

Don't fall for the lie! If you want to have victory through the tough times in this life, you cannot act like the teachings of Jesus don't matter. THEY MATTER! **Do not make them optional!** Work them into your day-to-day life and make them part of everything you do. You have to put in effort on a daily basis to work those teachings into your life and make them part of your foundation. You need to believe God's Word and be assured that what He said, He is also able to perform. Sometimes He'll do this through other people; other times He'll do it in an unexplainable, supernatural way, but He'll always do it.

The bottom line is this: If God said it, He can back it up. I'm building my life on that truth. I trust that as I hear His Word, believe it, and do what He says to do, then the hand of God will be upon my life. As storms come and go, my life (my house, so to speak), will not fall.

I pray you remember this and get it deep in your heart: Tough times don't last! There's nothing that God cannot do, cannot help, or cannot fix… **nothing!** There is nothing in this world that is locked that He cannot unlock, or show you the key. So stop telling God about your big problems. Start telling your problems about your big God… because tough times don't last! ↜

STARTING A NEW LIFE

If you've never asked Jesus Christ to be your Savior, you can invite Him into your heart by praying this simple prayer:

Father God, I come to You now, in Jesus' Name,

Jesus who loves me, and gave Himself for me.

Lord, I love You, and I give myself to You.

I ask You right now, come into my heart, come into my life,

be my Savior and be my Lord.

And by the blood of Jesus that was shed for me,

forgive me right now of every sin, cleanse me from all

unrighteousness, make me brand new.

And now, fill me with Your peace,

with Your joy, with the Holy Spirit,

and with the assurance that You'll never leave me,

and You'll never forsake me.

I thank You now, in Jesus' Name. Amen.

When you pray this prayer in faith, you are forgiven and made righteous by the blood of Jesus. Get rooted in a church that teaches the Bible. Continue to seek God and your faith will grow as your knowledge of God and His Word increases. ᕉ

ABOUT THE AUTHOR

*T*im Gilligan *founded non-denominational Meadowbrook Church in Ocala, Florida, in 1989. From humble beginnings, the church now has approximately 3,500 members, and continues to grow. Dedicated to sharing God's vision with his Meadowbrook family and an ever-expanding Internet audience, Pastor Tim teaches spiritual lessons with a blend of compassion, humor and above all, practical application.*

The author of several books, including Seasons, Playing for Keeps, Your Word and Your Work, *and* Transitions, *he also launched "The Life of Faith" broadcast in December 1998.*

Pastor Tim and his wife, Alicia, have raised five children and reside in Ocala. They enjoy spending time with their growing family, relaxing at home, visiting Florida attractions, and exploring country back roads in their Jeep.

To contact the author, please write to:

Meadowbrook Church

4741 S.W. 20th Street

Ocala, Florida 34474

352.873.3767

www.mbcocala.com

If your life has been impacted by reading this book, or if you have any questions, we encourage you to contact us. We look forward to hearing your testimony and welcome your prayer requests. We're praying for you and believe God is working in your life.